LIGHTS, CAMERA...**TRAVEL!**

ANDREW McCARTHY

Andrew McCarthy is a contributing editor at *National Geographic Traveler*. He's written for *The Atlantic*, *Travel + Leisure*, *Men's Journal*, *Slate*, *Afar*, *The Wall Street Journal*, and many other publications. In 2010 he was awarded the Lowell Thomas Award for Travel Journalist of the Year. As an actor, he's appeared in more than two-dozen films, including *Pretty in Pink*, *Less Than Zero*, *Weekend at Bernie's*, *The Joy Luck Club*, and *The Spiderwick Chronicles*. He has starred on Broadway *(Side Man)*, appeared often on TV *(Lipstick Jungle)*, and directed numerous television shows *(Gossip Girl)*.

DON GEORGE

Don George has edited five previous Lonely Planet literary anthologies, including *A Moveable Feast*, *The Kindness of Strangers* and *Tales from Nowhere*. He also wrote the *Lonely Planet Guide to Travel Writing*. Don has been global travel editor for Lonely Planet, travel editor at the *San Francisco Examiner & Chronicle* and founder and editor of Salon.com's *Wanderlust*. He is currently contributing editor and book review columnist for *National Geographic Traveler*, special features editor and blogger for Gadling.com and editor of the online literary travel magazine *Recce* (www.geoex.com/recce). Don appears frequently as a travel expert on television and radio and hosts a national series of on-stage conversations with prominent writers. He is also cofounder and chairman of the annual Book Passage Travel Writers and Photographers Conference.

LIGHTS, CAMERA...TRAVEL!

ON-THE-ROAD TALES FROM
SCREEN STORYTELLERS

EDITED BY

Andrew McCarthy
Don George

LONELY PLANET PUBLICATIONS

Melbourne • Oakland • London

Lights, Camera...Travel!
On-the-Road Tales from Screen Storytellers

Published by Lonely Planet Publications

Head Office:
90 Maribyrnong Street, Footscray, Vic 3011, Australia
Locked Bag 1, Footscray, Vic 3011, Australia

Branches:
150 Linden Street, Oakland CA 94607, USA
2nd floor, 186 City Rd, London, EC1V 2NT, UK

Published 2011

Printed in China
10 9 8 7 6 5 4 3 2 1

Copy edited by Victoria Harrison & Patrick Kinsella
Designed by Seviora Citra
Cover Design by Mark Adams

National Library of Australia Cataloguing-in-Publication entry

Lights, camera...travel! : on-the-road tales from screen storytellers / edited by
Andrew McCarthy & Don George.

ISBN 978 1 74220 493 2 (pbk.)

Travel -- Anecdotes.
Motion picture actors and actresses -- Travel.
Motion picture producers and directors -- Travel.
Screenwriters -- Travel.

McCarthy, Andrew.
George, Donald W.

910.4

Contents

Introduction

ANDREW McCARTHY
AND DON GEORGE

The premise behind this anthology is simple: since the ancient Greeks, actors have been society's storytellers. And ever since Hollywood first left the backlot, these storytellers have been traveling to far-flung corners of the world to tell those tales.

By necessity of the job, and often by nature, these 'Hollywood types' are a nomadic breed. Actors travel always with an eye and an ear – sometimes unconsciously, often deliberately – looking for characters, details of behavior, or inflections of voice, that can be logged away, stored for a future date, only to be recalled and employed for a role at the appropriate time. Writers move about listening for lines of dialogue that will unlock character, and directors bask in atmosphere in order to create a world on screen both specific and authentic. Most filmmakers will tell you that making a movie is easier on the backlot, but richer on the road.

We thought it would be illuminating – and entertaining – to ask some of these peripatetic storytellers to tell us their most personal, inspiring, funny, embarrassing and human stories from their time on the road. The result far surpassed our expectations: thirty-three tales by distinguished actors, directors and screen writers from around the world that are rich, raucous, and intimately revealing. While these stories are multifaceted in setting, voice and subject, one common theme threads through them: contact with the wider world through travel can delight, enlighten, inspire and change lives.

About half of these stories revolve around experiences related to a film. The other half recount travels not related to filming, in some case before careers even got started, in other cases in the troughs between triumphs, and in other cases on temporary career breaks.

In organizing these tales, we tried to follow both a chronological and a thematic structure. We begin with a couple of pieces that take place in the distant past – Alec Baldwin's wonderfully warm and wistful remembrance of Los Angeles, and Malcolm McDonald's poignant picturing of an epic journey he took as a youth around the world, accompanied by his flute and a friend named Floot.

These stories segue into further romantic remembrances set in Brazil, Australia and Hawaii. From there we present five stories that revolve around the theme of renewal – renewal through confronting the challenges of the road.

Beginning with Bill Bennett's evocative 'In Search of a Dolphin's Grave,' we present fourteen stories that focus on film-related experiences. Sitting around on set, actors, writers and directors often regale each other with stories of 'glory days' and famous mishaps – often with a showman's one-upmanship. Our tales capture this atmosphere: some recount adventures and discoveries encountered in the process of doing background research either for the writing of a script or for the making of a film; others focus on the rigors of filming in remote, often undeveloped places – and the unexpected riches and revelations that can result.

Introduction

For the last act in this multi-part epic, we present a suite of family stories – stories that explore themes of bonds made and broken, obstacles encountered and overcome, lessons learned, deaths endured and renewals nurtured. The final story in the book, Brett Paesel's extraordinary 'Life is a River in India,' beautifully illustrates the many-faceted gifts travel can bestow when we are open to and trusting in the world, our loved ones and ourselves.

Whether secure in a backlot or on distant location, working from a script or 'off book,' the storytellers in these stories ultimately reveal that they are just like us: human, full of foible, longing and grace – and that, just like us, when they venture into the wide world, that journey can touch and transform them.

LA Memories

ALEC BALDWIN

Alec Baldwin has appeared in over forty films, including *Beetle Juice*, *Working Girl*, *Miami Blues*, *The Hunt for Red October*, *Glengarry Glen Ross*, *Malice*, *The Juror*, *The Cooler* (National Board of Review Award for Best Supporting Actor; Oscar nomination), *The Aviator*, *The Departed* and *It's Complicated*. On television, Baldwin currently stars with Tina Fey in NBC's *30 Rock*, winner of three Emmy Awards for Outstanding Comedy Series (2007, 2008 and 2009). Baldwin has received five Screen Actors Guild Awards, three Golden Globe Awards, the Television Critics Association Award and two Emmy Awards as Best Actor in a Comedy Series for his performance on the show. He last appeared on stage in the 2010 Guild Hall (East Hampton) production of Peter Shaffer's *Equus*, directed by Tony Walton. Other stage performances include the Roundabout Theatre Company's 2006 production of Joe Orton's *Entertaining Mr Sloane*, directed by Scott Ellis; *Loot* (Broadway, 1986; Theatre World Award); Caryl Churchill's *Serious Money* (Broadway, 1988); *Prelude to a Kiss* (Circle Repertory Company, 1990; Obie Award); *A Streetcar Named Desire* (Broadway, 1992; Tony Award nomination); *Macbeth* (New York Shakespeare Festival, 1998); and *Twentieth Century* (Roundabout Theatre Company, 2004). He is also the author of *A Promise to Ourselves*, which was published in paperback in 2009. In 2011, Alec received his star on the Hollywood Walk of Fame.

LA Memories

Los Angeles has always been, well, a sore spot in my life. It might be safe to say that the bulk of the bad things in my life happened in LA, while the bulk of the good things happened in New York. It got so bad that I would feel a sense of personal defeat and demoralization whenever I landed there.

I've heard all of the analyses. My uncle Charles said that 'if you really are one in a million, then there are seven other people like you in New York City.' My friend Ken told me that New York is a river, with its own natural currents that seem to pull you in some direction, while LA is a lake. No currents. You've got to row where you want to go. Another said, 'LA will test everything you love, both friends and interests, because you gotta drive so far to get to them!' Another friend instructed me to find the outdoorsman in me. Take up hang-gliding. Hiking in the Angeles National Forest. I gravitated more toward the subway.

I heard more stuff like that. LA's not really a city but 'the chicest suburb in the world.' 'LA has great theater,' they would assure me. So-so pizza. The best sushi. The women. The movies. I have been one of the great LA haters of all time. That traffic. The San Diego Freeway, like some red carpet right into Hell. I recall driving my Karmann Ghia convertible north on the 405 in 1983, heading to an audition in Burbank, the air over the Valley like mustard gas, my eyes tearing. I remember reading in the *LA Weekly* that Santa Monica Bay was so contaminated from runoff that veteran lifeguards were developing cancers. I lived in Venice, full-time, 1983 through 1985. I couldn't wait to get out of there.

LA seems different to me now. Sure, old age has made me soften my view on a lot of things. But here's my LA, at least my memories of it. How I see it now.

>>>>>>>>>>>>>>>

My first apartment was on Larrabee, just north of Sunset. My friend and roommate, Tuck, and I had driven cross country in the Ghia in January and froze our asses off through the Texas panhandle. The place was around the corner from Spago. And the old Tower Records. I'd stand in Tower on some evenings for hours, wondering if I could ever earn enough money to buy all the music I wanted there. I fell in with a group of writers who worked for Garry Marshall. All from out of town. We would go to Lew Mitchell's Orient Express in the Miracle Mile district and eat 'gourmet Chinese food,' long before Mr Chow showed up. My friend Dana would order squab in lettuce cups. We'd go back to an apartment on Sunset Plaza Drive and drink and do all sorts of other illicit things late into the evening. In the morning we sobered up playing tennis at Dana's. Or Tuck and I would call the La Cienega Reservoir Courts and give a fake name to reserve a court. 'This is Dr Katz calling. I'd like a court at 11am.' The guy at the booth never even looked up at us when we checked in.

A few months later, Tuck and I moved to Venice. Sunset and Speedway. There was an empty, unpaved lot across from our apartment. Cars would insist on pulling into the soft sand and would get stuck there. People always asked us to call a tow truck for them. Late at night, cars would pull in that lot to party. We would throw eggs at them, ducking behind the wall of our second-story balcony like snipers, until they freaked out and left.

LA Memories

Monday mornings in Venice brought a fleet of municipal cleaning trucks. Giant sand-grooming devices that sifted out the trash and gave the beach an almost golf-course-type manicure. Another unit blasted benches that God-knows-what had leaked all over that weekend. I would walk to the Lafayette Café for the best *huevos rancheros* in California. The cooks were like noble Pancake Warriors who gazed at you with a faint smile. They knew they were cooking you the best and most honest meal you would ever have in your life. They knew that, at that moment, you needed that place. You knew it, too. The locals used to say that the old Venice died when 'the Laf' closed. It was my *Bright Lights, Big City* moment. The sound of the steaming jet of water that followed the disinfectant brushes on the wooden seats. The whirr of the sand behemoth. The birds savoring the last bit of trash before it was hauled away. The smell of the Laf and the stoic countenance of the Pancake Warriors.

Harry Perry on his rollerblades. The Figtree. The entrepreneur-freak called Jingles, who touched every base of the Venice Boardwalk Street Vendors Stations of the Cross. First he was a musician in a Sgt Pepper getup. Then a masseur. Then a palm reader. I think the only Venice gig he passed up was sketching portraits of Johnny Depp.

I moved back to New York after three years. I came back and met my ex-wife. Got married and moved to the Valley. Hated it. Then grew to love it for its lack of pretension. My ex and I would go to Malibu on weekends. Take Encinal Canyon for the long, verdant drive. We'd hit the chain of spots above Kanan Dume, the necklace formed by Matador, Pescador, La Piedra and Nicholas beaches, before the county paved the parking lots and put in meters. We'd sit on the bluff, looking down at the surfers at Nicholas, reading the Sunday *New York Times*. We'd hit Geoffrey's for dinner. The old Malibu Adobe. Moonshadows.

Neptune's Net, with all the bikers hanging out in their leathers in the sun.

Even now, I think about the great Mexican food at Tia Juana in West LA. Seeing an old movie at the New Beverly. Johnston's Yogurt Farm in Beverly Hills. The Getty, old and new. Patrick's Roadhouse. Madeo. Descanso Gardens. Duke's. Shopping for shirts at Citron on Montana. Tommy Tang's. Vine Street Bar and Grill. The Disney Concert Hall. Sitting on the shore at Zuma in November with a blanket wrapped around you. Now, when I drive up PCH, heading up near Leo Carillo for the sunset, I think ... I don't hate it here anymore. I don't hate it at all.

Me, Floot and the Flute

MALCOLM McDONALD

Malcolm McDonald transformed his early traveling passion for new people and places into a career (much to his delight and surprise), becoming a filmmaker whose projects have taken him to many exotic locations, from Costa Rica to North Africa to the Pacific Islands for *Family Footsteps* (Australian Broadcasting Commission) and *Lonely Planet 6 Degrees*. Lately he has concentrated on historical docudramas, including films on larger-than-life Australian characters such as Douglas Mawson, John Monash and William Buckley for ABC TV. He also worked as second unit director on Peter Weir's *Master and Commander*. Malcolm's films have been broadcast all over the world and have won numerous awards, including Australian Film Institute and ATOM awards for *Watch the Watch* (a film on hypnotism) and *Gumshoe* (on private detectives) and the Jules Verne Best Film and Director awards for *Mawson: Life and Death in Antarctica*. As life on the planet changes, Malcolm enjoys trying to document and understand it.

When you are young, in a strange land (Detroit, Michigan) in the early 1970s, staying with your aunt and wondering how to prolong the visit (as the food and board is a good change from the previous years' European working-backpacking routine so common with Australians overseas on their first pilgrimage), and you're drunk, standing at the top of the staircase of a Grosse Pointe country club at somebody's wedding, and you spy a girl down below – well, the answer could be beckoning. No, I didn't fall down the stairs! I glided down and fell in love.

Let's call her P. She had a semester to go for her degree at the University of Michigan in Ann Arbor (famous for its football team and the Rainbow People's Party, with frequent visits by John Lennon). She shared a big pea-green weatherboard house with students, and I shared her three-quarter-size bed in the room she shared with another girl.

Living in the house were a bunch of musicians, so while P was off at lectures I decided to learn the flute so I could play in their band. One of the guys played sax and flute and taught a very willing me – it was a full-on winter and I had six months to kill. One afternoon P and I were doing what you do when your roommate has a lecture, our passion ending with a rather high-pitched musical finish from the wondrous P.

At communal dinner that night one of the girls said, 'Man, you're getting really good on that flute.' I told them I hadn't played it all day and P chortled into her spaghetti. From then on P was called Floot!

When Floot graduated (with a psychology major – you need to know this), she and I went traveling in Europe in a

Volkswagen van we bought in Athens. We stayed with a family on the island of Skopelos for months as I started writing about my travels so far. Floot would make moussaka and carry it through the narrow whitewashed lanes to the baker and then be stopped constantly on her way home by all the women who would have a little look, touch and taste before commenting on her skills. Both of us loved going out with the fishermen at dawn – has barbecued octopus ever tasted better than in Greece?

We then went on to ski jobs in St Anton am Arlberg, Austria – me shivering all day on the lifts, Floot working as a housemaid in the home we were staying in. When she was asked to clean up the senile grandfather's shit, we decided life's too short!

As the van had Dutch plates we decided to go to Amsterdam to sell it. When we were twenty-three kilometers out, the police pulled us over, checked under the van and told us it was too rusty and they were going to take it to the nearest town and destroy it! Which they did! We caught the train to Amsterdam – which was especially memorable because when we walked in the door of a backpackers, that was the first time I heard Lou Reed's 'Walk on the Wild Side.'

That wonderful traveler's combo of places, people and songs. Unfortunately they played it over and over and over again ...

Having gotten no money for the van, we were almost broke, so Floot and I went back to Ann Arbor to look for work. We landed a job as houseparents in a halfway house for mentally disturbed women. Yes, we were only twenty-three and yes, Michigan had a progressive mental health policy. At any time there were eight patients ranging in age from seventeen to sixty, Floot and me (the only male). Some had tried to kill, some were young and abandoned, all were a constant challenge. I started writing about this extraordinary life and made up little plays, pertaining to their situation, for the women to perform. I learned a lot about women in our nearly two years there – but as I sit here many years later, I know that a lot is never really enough.

After this stint Floot and I decided to use the money we'd saved to travel overland from Istanbul to Australia, and off we set. Just about everywhere was open then on the so-called 'hippy trail' – how lucky we were – Iran, Afghanistan, Pakistan, the Hindu Kush, Kashmir, Burma, all accessible – not Vietnam as the war was still on, but Laos and Cambodia too.

I am so glad to have stood at the feet of the giant rock Buddhas of Bamiyan that the Taliban have since blown up, and I am almost glad to have taken a certain bus ride in Laos. We were going from Vientiane (a sleepy French colonial town then) to Luang Prabang (a very sleepy village). There were just locals on the bus. Somewhere in the mountains, within the bus – I can only describe it as an unspoken collective vibe – we all started to duck our heads, and then an automatic weapon strafed us, shooting out some windows, but we were all on the floor before the first shot hit. No-one was hurt – they said it was the Pathet Lao – but what intrigues me to this day is how we all felt it coming.

I had used the flute in Europe as the portable icebreaker that it is and was looking forward to joining with all the musical cultures that we would be meeting along the way. Before we left Ann Arbor, my teacher Sam told me that jazz musician Paul Horn had played his flute in the Taj Mahal and that each note stays for fourteen seconds. 'You need to do this for both of us,' he said (in E flat).

The first thing we noticed outside the entrance to the Taj Mahal was a sign saying 'NO FLUTE PLAYING!' These days I'm sure there's a flute-metal detector but then we were able to easily walk in with the flute in its pieces tucked away on our bodies. I assembled the flute as far away from the guards as possible and started playing Bach's Brandenburg Concerto No 2. I'll never forget those first sounds as the majestic echo of the dome kicked in. The guards came running of course – but then a wonderful thing happened. Lots of tourists pleaded with them, offering money – which they took and signaled that I could play for a few minutes. I was hearing so many notes (indeed chords) by this time that I started to play less and just jammed along with the echo – I'm smiling even now, remembering the gift of those precious moments.

We noticed a lot of fellow travelers were coming down with anything from dysentery to hepatitis. Floot and I had a rule that we would willingly eat all the street food but never drink the water (not even a fast-flowing Nepalese mountain stream). In those days at the end of a twenty-hour Afghani bus ride all you could get was warm Coke or Fanta – no bottled water. We used iodine tablets in a canteen, which tasted horrible, but in our whole trip Floot never got sick once and the only time I came undone was when I had severe runs while crossing from Afghanistan to Pakistan through the Khyber Pass! (Yes, the irony!) We were warned of rebels in the area, but I made the bus stop and ran over a hill to relieve myself. When I looked up from my grateful squat I saw men on the nearby ridge cradling guns and laughing themselves stupid. I ran back to the bus.

Sadly, another place you can't go today is the Swat valley in Pakistan. Floot and I took bus rides following the Swat River northwards. We never saw another Westerner till we came back down again. The dangerous rides had 'is it your time now' waiting around every corner as the road wound with the river, across rickety wooden suspension bridges. After a few days, Floot said, 'Have you noticed the further we go up the valley, each village has more and more men and they have henna in their hair and beards?' By the time we reached the top, into the Hindu Kush, these red-headed men made up about eighty per cent of the population at the last village we stayed in. I've never found an explanation.

Floot and I decided to take a cargo boat from Singapore to eastern Malaysia (three days of rank fish soup), then we took a rubber boat up the Rejang River in Sarawak because we'd heard that the Iban tribespeople (ex-headhunters) lived in huge longhouses on stilts and they welcomed you, if you just arrived there. We spent a night on the boat sleeping on squishy rubber slabs and then traveled all day to well into heart-of-darkness territory. In the late afternoon we got off onto a longhouse to puzzled looks from the Ibans and a grinning rubber boat captain as he went back down the river.

Nobody knew what to do – clearly we weren't very welcome – and we all just stood around in an uncomfortable no-language void. The longhouse was huge, all the village lived in it, over 500 people. It had wooden and bamboo sides and a thatched roof and went on forever. Floot was making some headway with sign language about the women's adornments when we heard the faint sound of a wooden flute. I took the flute case out of my pack and when I opened it there was a collective gasp from all around – the three silver pieces shone in the dying shafts of the sun and completely captivated the Ibans. I put it together and started to play something similar to what I was hearing. The astonishment surrounding me was just so sublime – the wonder of these silver sticks put together and now making music caught me up in that magic as well. People came running from everywhere and led us into the longhouse.

We had a very simple meal of fish and rice as the longhouse was lit with candles and lamps. After dinner, musicians assembled with flutes and various percussive instruments and drums and we played together and Floot danced with the women – she looked so beautiful in the golden light. When it was time for bed we were given a spot near a major support pole and left alone.

After a time a man walked by and pointed up at the top of the pole and went on his way. Floot and I took the tip and found footholds and climbed to the top and sat on crossbeams. From there we could see the whole longhouse – families separated by hessian curtains. We stayed up there for hours watching the comings and goings – hearing the soundscape of babies, lovers, snorers – feeling the nightly pulse of the village.

After traveling through seventeen countries over nearly two years we made it to Bali.

Floot's brother was getting married back in Michigan and her mother had arranged a flight out of Bali for her – I think fearing that if she made it to Australia she might be gone forever. Even Kuta beach was not much more than a collection of shacks then, and that's the Bali I like to remember.

I went on to Australia and became a filmmaker.

I still have the flute, but never play it – the last time it was played was by my niece at her grandfather's funeral.

And Floot? Ah, well, that's another story.

Dolphin Love:
A Brazilian Romance

DANA DELANY

Dana Delany has been nominated for five Emmys and won two for *China Beach*. She has also appeared in the films *Tombstone, Light Sleeper* and *Route 30*, the TV shows *Desperate Housewives, Pasadena, True Women* and *Wild Palms*, and the plays *Dinner with Friends* and *Translations*. She can currently be seen in *Body of Proof* on ABC and in the film *Freelancers* with 50 Cent. Her passions are acting, art and travel. Send her a first class ticket and she'll meet you anywhere.

Dolphin Love: A Brazilian Romance

It was 1985 and I had just moved to Los Angeles to perform in a play at a tiny theater in Santa Monica. I had done the play off Broadway in New York and the playwright, Nick Kazan, had graciously asked me to be in the LA production. I thought, why not? I actually got to arrive in Hollywood with a job.

And it got even better. Several casting people came to see the play and after several auditions I landed a job in a movie. Not just any movie. One that was shooting in Brazil. I have loved travel since I was a child. I still get excited arriving curbside at any airport. It doesn't matter that one has to deal with security or lines or people in sweatpants. I'm going somewhere! And that to me means romance and adventure.

The movie was called *Where the River Runs Black*. It was based on a Brazilian legend about a little boy who is the child of a beautiful young woman and a pink dolphin. I guess that would be the true outcome of 'dolphin love.' The boy was raised wild in the Amazon and can swim like a, well, dolphin. I was to play a nun in the orphanage where the boy is taken.

Flying to Brazil on Varig airline was the height of luxury. And I was *Flying Down to Rio!* It was everything I dreamed of – movies, exotic locations, first class! We changed planes and took a smaller one to Belém, which is the capital of the state of Pará and sits at the mouth of the Amazon. When I got off the plane and walked across the tarmac, I experienced what would later get me my next job in Brazil a year later with Paul Mazursky. 'When you get off the plane, the heat goes right to your crotch,' I told him. And it did.

I have since heard that Belém has had a building boom and become quite urban, but that would come later. In 1985, it was still a sleepy colonial town with beautiful mango trees and quite a bit of poverty. I had never experienced that kind of begging on the streets, despite having lived in New York. But Belém was teeming with life and vibrancy. And even innocence. Because it was so humid, the local people wore very little clothing, but what they wore was colorful and almost childlike. And there were children everywhere. It was a town filled with families. I saw mothers lead their young children to the edge of the sidewalk to pee in the street. And no-one cared. It was quite remarkable and liberating.

The actors were staying at the American Hilton, which was an air-conditioned oasis in the Amazon because you really couldn't last more than an hour in the heat. The Hilton had a dark bar and an oval pool. It turned out that I would be working very little on this movie over the course of a month, so I had some free time, which suited me just fine. I was blessed to be working with Charles Durning (playing a priest), who is a world-class dancer. He taught ballroom dancing in New York after World War II. We would go out for *feijoada* and *caipirinhas* and then dance. I have never met a man who could dance a samba with such delicacy. During the day, I took trips to the seaport where the wharf was stocked with seafood fresh off the boat. One weekend I went to Ilha de Marajó, a small island that sits exactly where the Amazon River meets the Atlantic Ocean. I was happily sunbathing nude on the sugary sand when I heard a rushing noise. The Atlantic tide was coming in and threatening to drown me at a rapid pace. I quickly doggie-paddled to higher land with my clothes over my head. Just part of the adventure of Brazil.

But the most romantic one was yet to come. I spent a good deal of my time by the pool at the Hilton, waiting to hear if I would work that day. I lay in the sun (on the equator, mind you) in my leopard-print Norma Kamali one-piece ready to quickly don my nun's habit. It was the tannest I have ever been in my life and the last time I would ever sunbathe. What was I thinking? I blame it on Rio. Or Belém.

One afternoon I glanced up from my book and saw a Greek god complete with tousled golden hair walk out to the pool and lie down on a chaise. I went back to my book. Then he got up to go in the pool and I lost my place. I noticed that he had left an open book with his towel. I casually got up to see what language he was reading in. It was English and he was reading *Ulysses* by James Joyce. Who reads that at a pool? He got out of the water and I scooted back to my chaise. When he gathered his things to leave, I decided that if he walked towards me I would say something, otherwise it was not meant to be.

I regret to say that my opening line was weak: 'Where are you from?'

'Ireland.'

'Really? You don't sound Irish.'

'You should hear me after a couple of pints of Guinness.'

'Ha ha ha.'

I can't remember if he suggested the drink in the bar later or I did. I hope it was he.

When I arrived, freshly showered, I saw him standing at a distance, in a blue Oxford cloth shirt at the bar, and I actually gasped. It was my 'Hubbell' (from *The Way We Were*) moment. We sat, ordered drinks and started to ask questions. It turned out that he was traveling solo through the Amazon on a motorcycle. It was his Indiana Jones fantasy. Belém was his last stop before he headed to Rio and then back to school.

I said, 'School? How old are you?'

'Twenty-one.'

'Oh my God.'

'Why, how old are you?'

'Twenty-nine.'

'What? I thought you were sixteen. The cheek of this girl to pick me up.'

Thus started my lifelong relationship with younger men.

Cameron was on break from Oxford and due back in a couple of weeks. He was indeed Irish, well-known Irish, as his father was a very successful businessman. We spent the next few days enjoying Belém together. As I said, the city had a wonderful mix of innocence and eroticism and it was the same with my movie location romance. We went to a local carnival and rode the Ferris wheel. I remember sitting at the top, looking over the lights of the city, thinking life can't get much sweeter than this. Or stranger. One of the local highlights was a wooden roadhouse where all the families went on Saturday night. There was a big boombox, and young girls would get up and perform dances to hits like Paul Young's 'Every Time You Go Away,' which was popular at the time. And then they would take their clothes off. Completely. And the families would applaud. I think maybe it was a whorehouse on the side.

And of course we knew it would end, like all movie romances must, which made it even sweeter. He went to Oxford via Rio and I finished the movie as a very tan nun. It was everything I had fantasized about as a child. Exotic location, romance with a handsome stranger who rode out of the jungle on a motorcycle, and a chance to act with Charles Durning! Little did I know that most of my foreign locations to come would be in Canada. Not that it isn't a lovely country.

Postscript: Cameron and I did stay in touch. I spent Christmas with his family in Ireland and we dated for a while. He is now happily married and we spoke just last spring. Brazil is still one of my favorite countries to visit today.

Honeymooning with Sharks

RICK MARIN

Rick Marin started out as a journalist before taking up film and television. He wrote a bestselling memoir, *Cad: Confessions of a Toxic Bachelor,* and has worked at the *New York Times* and *Newsweek*. He lives in Los Angeles with his wife and writing partner, Ilene Rosenzweig, and their two boys, Diego and Kingsley.

*T*hwaaackk!
A fresh swath of blood smeared the whitewashed walls of our jungle hideout.

'Got him!' Ilene exclaimed, standing on a rattan chair in the lingerie of a paid assassin.

That was *my* blood. The bastard. He deserved to die.

'Kill them all!' I commanded, cowering under the bedclothes while my newlywed bride re-rolled her copy of *Hello!*, took aim at a mosquito the size of a Prius and ... *spplaaaat!*

Did I mention I have a crazed fear of mosquitoes? They're my Room 101 (*1984* – look it up). If I hear them whining in my ear, I go mental. Their bites turn into enormous welts. They crave my flesh. When we showed up at this rain forest eco-resort on Australia's Daintree River, it had just poured for nine straight days and the 'mozzies' were out in force. The moment we arrived, the resort director hosed us down with industrial-strength DEET. Or napalm. Whatever toxic pesticide they freely use to ward off the bloodsucking pests that have plagued this land since the Aborigines owned the place.

I wondered: when Nietzsche wrote 'That which does not kill me makes me stronger,' was he honeymooning in Australia? Or was he already mad with syphilis by then?

After the logistical and emotional D-day of a wedding, most newlyweds are content to lie on a beach, high on postnuptial bliss, umbrella drinks and what a friend of mine calls the 'Jamaican vegetable.'

Not my wife.

We got married in Italy. At a sixteenth-century abbey outside Portofino. We could have hopped a train to Tuscany for two weeks. But no. We had to fly halfway around the world for an 'Extreme Honeymoon' that would test not only our marriage, but my role in it as, well, the Man.

Ilene had always been hard to get. That was her rep and it had taken my full repertoire just to persuade her to go on a date, much less spend the rest of our lives together. But it worked. She was wearing the ring. Well, she actually wasn't, but that's another story. This Extreme Honeymoon thing felt like the final test, even though we were *already married.*

'Come on,' she coaxed. 'It'll be more fun.'

'Yeah, sure. Fun.'

I knew what was going on here. A template was being set. A gauntlet dropped. Every hotel we stayed at, every adventure we booked, I took as a challenge to my manhood. The sexual dynamics. Power struggles. Gender role-playing. Could I provide? Could I protect? Could I ... *represent*? This was how it was going to be for the next thirty, forty ... fifty years. Was I a guy who could tough out the inevitable trials of a shared life and family – for richer or poorer, in sickness and in health? Or was I going to cower under a musty, malarial comforter at the slightest sign of trouble?

Add to these nerve-racking existential stakes the fact that I was on a book tour for my memoir, *Cad: Confessions of a Toxic Bachelor*. The book had just come out in Australia. I was writing the screenplay for Miramax. If we were going to be there anyway, I figured, why not do a little publicity? Cheesy, yes. But an author will stop at nothing to move the merch.

So here we were, flip-flopping around the most lethal continent on the planet. My wife, the thrill-seeker. Me, the safety-seeker. I remember it all like the fever dream it seemed at the time.

>>>>>>>>>>>>>>>

'How're you going?'

This was the concierge at The Establishment, a boutique hotel in Sydney. Our first stop in the land of Oz. She was about six-foot-five – your standard Australian supermodel/triathlete/surf goddess.

'Great!' I replied. 'How am I going *where*?'

It took me a week to get used to this stock Ozzie salutation. If you mean, 'How are you doing?' why don't you bloody well say it?

But I wasn't here to argue linguistics. I was here to pass the first test. The Room Test.

Ours was small and dark, with no view. Ilene said it was 'fine,' in a way that suggested I better fucking upgrade us before she got back from the salon. Yeah, that was just a little pressure as I stood there in the Establishment lobby looking up, *way* up, at this Aussie Glamazon. I'm not a room-changer, okay. I'm Canadian. We say thank you to ATMs. But I knew I couldn't face my bride in the same cramped cell she'd left me in.

I informed Elle Macpherson's hotter sister that my wife and I were on our honeymoon and braced myself for the standard boutique-hotel stonewall. Instead, she handed over a key to ... the Penthouse. The – *wink* – 'Robbie Williams Suite.' He'd just stayed there, she said, with a coy smile. 'Enjoy it.'

'Thanks,' I said, a little stunned by the pair I'd just grown. 'We will.'

When Ilene got back, I welcomed her to our loft-like aerie, where we partied like overblown British pop stars for the rest of our stay in Sydney.

I passed the first test. But we had yet to embark on the 'extreme' portion of our antipodal adventure.

>>>>>>>>>>>>>>

Lizard Island is an exclusive, no-kids getaway whose claims to fame are: 1) Captain Cook scaled the island's peak to survey the treacherous shoals that were foundering his ships; and 2) it's forty-five minutes by boat from the Great Barrier Reef.

I tried to climb 'Cook's Look' to impress Ilene, and it damn near killed me. We were halfway up – me huffing, puffing, ready to turn back – when this 60-year-old from Adelaide who'd killed me on the tennis court the day before ran past *on his way down*. This is what you're dealing with down here. Perfect, retirement-age specimens of manhood who play soccer three times a week and complain about 'slowing down.'

The next day we were on the boat out to the Great Barrier Reef for a little snorkeling. No scuba. I don't enjoy 'sports' where there's a chance you might have an embolism and die. I might have skipped the boat ride altogether, but I sensed this was another test.

So I hunkered down in the cabin, where any sane person would be given the size of the waves, the speed of the boat and the fact that the captain looked like a human pint of Foster's. Oh, and I had forgotten my inhaler. What if I had an asthma attack in the middle of a school of barracuda? Ilene had disappeared. I looked around and saw her at the front of the boat – the prow? the bow? whatever the fuck it's called – having a *Titanic*-style tête-à-tête with Stefano, the Italian dive instructor.

Nice. On our honeymoon. I had no choice. I put on a life jacket – the boat going *bump, splash, bump, bump* – and inched along the guardrail, white-knuckled, to confront my beloved bride.

'What, you didn't get enough swarthy, effortlessly stylish Euro-guidos defiling you with their eyes at the *wedding*?'

She looked at me, salt air whipping my face, touched by my jealousy. 'I was just telling Stefano to keep an eye on you in the water. You seemed worried about your inhaler.'

The strapping Italian grinned. He clearly hadn't understood a word.

The engines cut out and our boat sat bobbing like a bathtub toy on the edge of the fathomless depths of the Pacific Ocean. I put on my mask and fins and splashed over the side with the other tourists. Stefano stayed close as we gazed down into the wonders of the reef. Totally nice guy. Incredible abs. Just as I was getting lost in the bromance of it all came the terrified, flailing cry:

'*Shark!*'

Not from me. It was Ilene. She'd just noticed the three-foot sand sharks brushing the floor of the reef. I'd seen them, too, but figured they were too small to worry about. As Stefano reassured Ilene, I dived down for a closer look. My wife was already back on the boat, shivering.

I wasn't keeping score, but I won that one.

>>>>>>>>>>>>>>>

Australia boasts seven of the world's ten deadliest snakes. When my half-sister moved here she reported scorpions in her backyard. We drove past miles and miles of pristine beaches that were completely empty because of the presence of 'stingers' – jellyfish the size of your thumbnail capable of inflicting excruciating pain. You don't die, but you wish you would.

I guess living every day with the possibility that something could kill you is what built up the bravado and cavalier machismo Australians are known for. And it's not just the men.

We'd just come out of a toad-racing event in Port Douglas – what, you haven't been to one of those? – and were dodging the massive swooping brown bats known as flying foxes when Ilene got into an altercation with some drunk townie tarts.

Parts of Queensland are Australia's equivalent of the Ozarks. The men sit in bars on whose every wall hangs a television set broadcasting some form of gambling, or Australian Rules Football. (Punch line: there *are* no rules!) The women have a hard, ropey look – with their tight black jeans and accents that could cut glass. So here we were, minding our own business, when the words 'American cunt' were uttered. I'm not sure they realized who they were dealing with: a Jewish girl from Long Island. But I sensed it wasn't going to end well. I really should have stepped in, but those chicks looked strong and I felt a *Deliverance* moment coming on. So I pulled us into the cab that the ropey tarts accused us of stealing from them and averted an international crisis. Or YouTube sensation.

I will say this for the Australian ladies. In America, Canada, and the UK, I'd been pilloried by many a female reviewer for the 'toxic bachelor' behavior recounted in my memoir. But here, the reaction of the women who interviewed me for the local papers, radio or TV was: 'He's not so bad!' Compared to the knuckle-draggers they were used to, I was a softie. Barely a cad at all. After all, the whole reason I was here was to honeymoon with the book's happy ending. How bad could I be?

>>>>>>>>>>>>>>

Our last 'extreme' act before flying back to reality as husband and wife was to go 'abseiling' in the Blue Mountains, an hour or so outside Sydney. You get into a harness and rappel down the mountainside. Again, Ilene's idea. As soon as she looked over the edge, she wanted to go home. But the guys who took us had a company motto: 'Feel the Fear, But do it Anyway.' It's on their T-shirts.

I went first, to show her it was no biggie. The ninety-eight-foot drop was easy, like a climbing wall. She made it down, too. Shaken, but too proud not to go to the next level. The 197-foot. I went first again. It was awesome. Ilene followed. Afterward, she looked a little green. 'You don't have to go,' I said.

'No, I want to.'

I zipped down. Totally ninja. Now it was Ilene's turn. She was taking so long the wind had kicked up. My newlywed bride was buffeted across the cliff like a rag doll. The instructors steadied her rope, told her to keep going. They were yelling. I was yelling. It took a while, but she made it down, flushed, trembling and fell into my arms. After two weeks of feeling like Quentin Crisp in this land of He-Men, and He-Women, it felt good to look macho in her eyes. To be the guy she could lean on.

So *this* was the template we forged on our honeymoon. One of us pushes the other to do something extreme or risky that the other would never have done on his or her own and we're both the better for it.

It's been that way ever since. Australia's fatal shores, booby-trapped jungles and brazen locals gave us a motto to face marriage, and life, by.

Feel the fear, but do it anyway.

Seven years later, I still have the T-shirt.

Island Love

DANI KLEIN MODISETT

Dani Klein Modisett is a writer and actress who created the live show *Afterbirth ... Stories You Won't Read in a Parenting Magazine*. An anthology of stories from the show was published by St Martin's Press. Dani spent the previous ten years working as an actress on Broadway, in movies and television and as a comic before settling down in Los Angeles with her husband. She is a frequent contributor to *Parents* magazine and recently created a new show, *Not What I Signed Up For*, which tackles the subject of marriage with the same candor and wit that *Afterbirth* uses to shed light on the truth about being parents. Dani has two young sons and is a graduate of Dartmouth College.

'Your parents never took you to Hawaii?' a man with graying temples asked me with the same gravity you might inquire about a person's childhood spent bouncing from foster home to foster home. It was June and my husband Tod and I were at his prep school reunion. I was in no mood for being pitied for never having been taken to a tropical island. I had pity covered, self-pity to be exact, having spent a fruitless year trying to have a second child. Since Tod and I had depleted not only our spirits, but our family nest egg trying to get pregnant again, hearing how underprivileged my life had been for not taking a vacation that I would not be taking any time soon was enough to make me stick my tongue under the chocolate fountain on the dessert table.

'That guy's always been an ass,' Tod said on the drive home, as I drifted in and out of a sugar coma.

'I'll take you to Hawaii, honey,' he added, pushing aside a piece of hair matted to my cheek by brown dots.

The next day while Gabriel, our nineteen-month-old, slept, I googled 'Hawaii hotels.' Through a series of finger taps I landed on the Mandarin Oriental on O'ahu. I couldn't take my eyes off the synchronized dolphins swimming in and out of gleaming blue water to the sounds of Hawaiian folk music. I so wished I could blink and be there. Too bad I wasn't *Bewitched,* and we were flat broke.

'We should go,' Tod said, looking at my screen as he headed into the bedroom to see if Gabriel had woken up from his nap.

'Yeah, right,' I said, leaning back in my chair still mesmerized by the islands. Sure, I thought, let's make some money out of air and take a Hawaiian vacation. Then when we come home all rested and refreshed I can take Gabriel to work with me at Starbucks so at least we'll have free coffee to drink.

Tod came back in, Gabriel in his arms still drunk with sleep until he heard my voice and reached for me.

'Momma! Momma! I want Momma!'

I guess pleasuring oneself into a cup for almost a year and feeling helpless to make your wife happy can move a man to irrational actions because Tod made good on his promise. He took whatever money we had left, and some of what we didn't, and decided to take his adorable son and very tired wife away for some much-needed renewal and rebuilding of the family. Especially now that it was clear that it was just going to be the three of us. So there we were at the gate of an airplane headed over the Pacific, tagging Gabriel's stroller to be safely stored below.

'This is fucking crazy, Tod,' I said, struggling to fold up the stroller and get it on the plane.

'I know. They really should make those easier to collapse.'

'I don't mean the stroller,' I said, snapping it locked with my finger inside.

'I know what you meant,' Tod said, smiling. 'But you deserve it,' he added, disengaging my throbbing pinkie. 'We deserve it. Honestly, we need it. And it's a done deal so you might as well try to enjoy it. '

'Mommy, booby,' Gabriel said, tugging on the front of my shirt.

'Okay, honey, on the plane,' I said, leaning over, trying not to flash my fellow travelers.

'*Aloha*, ladies and gentlemen. All passengers with small children are now invited to board flight 357 to Honolulu.'

Since Gabriel decided to party down with an in-flight five-hour nursing fest, by the time the plane's wheels touched the tarmac I was pretty sore, and if possible, even more exhausted.

He had fallen asleep for about ten minutes, but then managed to wake up just in time for the landing. All he could do was point to his ears and scream while Tod hustled to get our items together and relieve the people around us from his wailing.

'I know you said something about trying to enjoy myself, but really ... ' I said, holding Gabriel on my hip while trying to slam the stroller open this time. As I stood up from fastening him in to his seat, an unfamiliar tan hand came around my neck and lightly brushed my sensitive breast, dropping a ring of fresh-cut orchids around my neck. It smelled like hibiscus flowers and coconut.

'*Aloha*, madame, welcome to Hawaii. Let me help you.'

Just then Tod returned from the bathroom.

'I just got lei-ed, honey.'

'That's great. And you're blushing.'

'Right this way please, my friends,' my savior said, his hand near the small of my back guiding us in the right direction.

>>>>>>>>>>>>>>

As soon as we get outside, the moisture in the air makes my skin tingle. There's a clammy, squishy, wet quality to the atmosphere that feels nurturing in a way that the southern California desert never will. A minibus is waiting to take us to the hotel. Before boarding, another strand of orchids is draped around my neck. '*Aloha*, madame,' the bus driver says.

'*Aloha* to you,' I say, not sure how to respond to his kind face. Tod stands behind me smiling.

'Momma, come on! Bus! Bus!' Gabriel says, grabbing my hand and pulling me up the few steps to our seats. We pick up about six other people on our way to the hotel. Each passenger joining us is more attractive than the last. All are dressed in flowing, colorful resortwear that looks like it can come off with the release of one hook or the unfastening of a single button. I've been using my body (and Tod's) as a tool of science for so long now that I've forgotten how beautiful, graceful, fluid and hot the human form can be. And it turns out that people who vacation in Hawaii are very attractive specimens indeed. They smell good, too, like fresh-cut flowers and almond oil and success.

Walking into the lobby of the Mandarin Oriental Hotel on O'ahu, I feel like I should be a queen or at least have had my hair blown out. It's a huge open space, with lovely oriental detailing, flooded with light and anchored by a massive chandelier at its center. And bars serving fruity drinks on either end. We decide to sit and have a few before going up to the room. Gabriel runs around us in circles, stopping every once in a while to pick a nut out of the bamboo bowl on the table between Tod and me. A man in white pants stands before us to take our order. I don't usually like men in white, but since we are sitting and he is standing within reach, if you will, it is hard not to notice how nicely he wears them.

'Honey, you're staring,' Tod says.

'What? At his ivory cuff links. Please. They're clearly a hand job. I mean handmade. They're handmade!' I say, giggling.

What is happening to me, I think. I am supposed to be depressed.

'Handmade!' Gabriel yells, imitating me, grabbing a macadamia nut. We sign for the check and head to our room.

'If you need anything at all, my name is Kai,' the porter says a few minutes later at the room, wheeling in our bags.

'Okay, Kai, thank you,' I say, handing him a tip, thinking he must be related to our waiter and wondering what strange universe this is where everyone is so gracious and handsome. I wonder if it's hard to get a job here and if they have any openings for women who used to be funny.

Our spacious room is lushly appointed with shiny, soft fabrics, glossy Hawaiian magazines and lightly scented candles. It has a huge window overlooking the ocean. The king-size bed is piled high with pillows, and covered in 400-count Pima cotton sheets. The bathroom is stocked with thick, soft towels, and has a deep bathtub with a jar of almond salt on a slate ledge for you to pour in the water with the help of a small seashell. There's even a welcome basket just for kids with baby shampoo, a few small ceramic turtles, and three size-three diapers. These are too small for Gabriel, but in a pinch, a diaper is a diaper. A crib sits by the window as requested.

I am standing in the lap of luxury – but for one small detail. Even though I am certain Tod and I will never engage in sex again that isn't premeditated, scheduled, and then analyzed for effectiveness, if perchance we do want to break free for a little wild island action here, clearly we'll be doing it with Gabriel as our audience. Despite the hotel's royal hospitality, it appears no-one has considered where, when or how we are to express our reawakened passion with a toddler right by our side.

I check the closets to see if the crib will fit in any of them, which is probably against the law, but it's not like we'd make him sleep there overnight. None is big enough. All right, I think, this isn't meant to be a sex trip anyway, this will be an at-least-I-don't-feel-hopeless-anymore-because-I-can-always-move-to-Hawaii-and-be-a-chambermaid vacation. As for the hotel, no matter how posh, it clearly is not their job to anticipate guests' nooky needs.

We unpack, take a quick tour of the pools, including the one where dolphins live, enjoy a few glasses of wine and some chicken nuggets with pineapple sauce, watching the sunset, and decide to retire early. Nothing sounds more delicious than the sounds of the ocean lulling me to sleep in that big, soft bed.

'Momma! Momma! I don't like it here!' Gabriel is still screaming three hours later. Tod had given up and passed out reading his *New Yorker* at hour one. He doesn't even pretend that he can comfort his young son the way Mommy can and most of the time I don't hold it against him. Tonight I am not feeling quite so generous. I finally take Gabriel out of his crib and bring him to bed with me and we both pass out.

I hear rustling in the morning and pretend to be asleep.

'Hey, buddy, let's let Momma sleep,' Tod whispers, 'and go get some eggs together and see the dolphins!'

'Dolphins! Dolphins!' Gabriel yells. I take shallow breaths until I hear the door click behind them.

I lie still for a minute in fantastic silence but then quickly decide I should assume this exact position out by the pool, in full vacation mode. I pull on my bathing suit, which fits as tight as a condom, avoid the full-length mirror, and tie a scarf around my ass as a faux sarong and head downstairs. I find a vacant chair conveniently placed directly across from a young man who had caught my eye yesterday. His skin is evenly tanned and he has dark eyes and thick, wavy hair. He wears a rawhide string tied in a knot at his wrist that I find myself wanting to bite. His cutoff shorts rest on his sinewy hipbones like he's just waiting for someone to pull them off.

Why not me, I think, smiling to myself and looking around for a drink. How about because he looks about eighteen and you just left forty in the dust and are here on your first family vacation, Mrs Robinson? Looking at this boy in this way should make me feel guilty. It doesn't. It makes me feel sexy. Pre-marriage-and-kids sexy. Hungry for the kind of sex the kids chase. Sure, baby-making sex has all the exchange of bodily fluids and friction of sexy sex, but absolutely none of the carefree, illicit, crazy passion of, say, sex with a handsome, sullen, tan boy on a beach in the tropics.

I readjust the incline of my chair, lie back, and run a hand through my hair. I wonder if he's noticed me in the twenty-four hours we've been here together. The smoldering brunette with the sore nipples from breastfeeding a toddler. I close my eyes, take a deep breath and float myself back in time, until I, too, am eighteen. He and I meet over a chilled glass of cucumber/strawberry/lemon/pineapple/mint water at the sparkly gym with the wall of glass showcasing a vast expanse of the Pacific. We've made contact a few minutes before, looking up from our individual television screens placed conveniently at eye level on every cardio machine. I hold my gaze with him just long enough to say, 'I'm in.' He pours me a cup of water from the sterling-silver dispenser without even asking if I want any. I take it, looking directly into his cocky brown eyes. We stand together, breathing, sweating, recovering, about to speak, and then I hear it.

'Mommy! Mommy! Come see, come see the big fish, Mommy!' My eyes fly open and like Cinderella at midnight, everything changes. My laugh lines return to my face, my breasts head south, my heart swells and I see Tod and Gabriel running toward me.

Gabriel is ahead with Tod's arms reaching out to grab him before he tumbles into the pool. 'Hi guys! How was it?' I ask, blocking the sun with my hand, and moving my head slightly, shaking my illicit thoughts away like dry sand.

'I think he's really asleep,' I say to Tod back in the room that night after another dinner al fresco.

'Cool,' Tod says, from the bed. 'Come up here, you little hula dancer.'

I took a free hula dance lesson on the beach while Gabriel napped today and loved it. I quietly hum a few bars of a Don Ho hit and climb up next to him.

He kisses me softly on the lips, untying the string at the top of the bathing suit I'm still wearing. The triangles of fabric fall away and he pulls me toward him. I remember the citrus and cinnamon smell of his neck and the way Tod always holds me with purpose and sink further into his arms.

'Momma? Momma. Momma!!!!'

>>>>>>>>>>>>>>>

I feel sunlight on my face streaming through a crack in the curtains the next morning and open my eyes. After six consecutive hours of sleep I feel like a new woman. I am, however, desperate for a latte. Since the boys are still asleep I dress quickly and sneak downstairs to the Hoku's restaurant. It's the fancy one at the resort so I know they'll have good coffee and hopefully *malasadas* to bring back to Gabriel. He had one of these puffy fried balls of dough dipped in sugar yesterday and went to sleep, the second time last night, talking about them.

'I just heard the guys outside talking about record waves on the island. Is it true?' I ask the waitress as she steams my milk.

'Fifty-foot waves on the North Shore this morning,' she says. 'A couple of the bus boys got up early to drive up and see them. You should go. But leave early because it'll be a mob scene.'

'Oh, wow. We have to go!' I say. I want to see live surfing while we are here since I never have. I take Gabriel's bag of donuts and get back to our room as quickly as I can. When I open the door, he and Tod are running around laughing raucously over made-up names for the clay turtles.

'Get dressed, we're going to see the biggest waves ever!'

'Get dressed!' Gabriel says to Tod, mimicking me, and cramming the sweet dough in his mouth.

'Okay,' says Tod.

'Okay!' yells Gabriel.

We get to the most desirable wave-watching area and people are standing ten deep for as far as the eye can see. I'm feeling distracted because I'm worried that this is not the safest place for Gabriel and that we're running out of sunscreen – until I see the first colossal wave heading toward the shore. In a matter of seconds we're watching a wall of water rise up out of the ocean as if being pulled by God. The three of us grab hands and stare, transfixed, looking at surfers the size of fleas catching these waves until they break and fall back into the ocean with a thunderous crash. I look at Gabriel's face and although he can't say it with words, it is clear that he has just learned the meaning of awesome.

All the excitement and lack of sleep over the last few days has caught up with him and inching along the coast back to the hotel, Gabriel falls asleep in his car seat.

'Wow,' I say to Tod, 'it really is so beautiful here.'

'Yep,' Tod says.

'So that guy at your reunion isn't a total ass, I mean, at least he has good taste.'

'Like me,' Tod says, taking my hand. 'It's good we did this, right?'

'Yes, it is,' I say, kissing him on the ear. 'Thank you.'

Gabriel is still asleep when we transfer him out of the car and wheel him up to the room in his stroller. Tod drops him in the darkest corner of the room and takes the dolphin-shaped chocolate off our pillow. He unwraps it, takes a bite and places the other half in my mouth. We lie down on the bed together savoring the rich taste and the quiet. We kiss, pulling each other's clothes off like the old days.

Only better.

Boarding the plane at the end of our trip, I keep thinking about four words I read on a cocktail napkin in the lobby when we first arrived at the hotel. '*Aloha aku, aloha mai,*' on one side. 'Give love, get love,' on the other.

Two weeks after we land back in Los Angeles, I find out I'm pregnant.

And not by a teenager.

Through Jordan and Syria

JOSH LUCAS

Josh Lucas was born in the early 1970s in Arkansas and spent his childhood traveling with his activist parents who organized anti-nuclear protests all over the South. The family finally settled in a small fishing village in Washington State, where Josh's small public school had a nationally ranked, award-winning debating and drama program. He has been traveling and acting ever since.

To be blunt, this 'entertainment industry' I have spent over twenty years working in can kick your ass. In the early winter of 2010, I find myself metaphorically lying in the mud, bloody and bruised, and with a nasty headache. The beautiful promise of a great career job has just blown past me, knocking me viciously to the ground. Rejected, I realize that I've taken this loss way too hard and that my perspective is off. So I decide a solo trip to somewhere I've never been is what I need to get my head together. Wanting a total immersion outside of my comfort zone, I choose the Middle East.

A few days later, I land in Israel. A sleepless zombie, I whisk breezily through the world's most secure airport. Exiting customs, I feel confused as all my research has prepared me for a cavity search or at the very least a serious interrogation, and here I stand in Israel without anyone having had even a peek at my belongings.

I take a public bus to the closest stop near the old city of Jerusalem. I enter through Damascus Gate and instantly the ancient market engulfs me in color, sensation, and smells. I'm joyfully overwhelmed, lost for a while in the maze of the old city. I reach the Muslim quarter and quickly leave my bags in the 500-year-old marble-floored hostel I'm staying in. Then I walk into the corridor and find myself uttering 'Oh my God,' my mouth literally agape as I fall from experience to experience. I wander through the mass of spirituality and emotion that is boiling inside this mind-blowing human creation honoring God: Jerusalem. There is no doubt about the presence of God here. I also feel utter madness. It is instantly obvious to me why this place causes war and death. And salvation.

Needing to breathe, I head back into the market to a café where I've scheduled a meeting with Philip, an African-born, French-raised Jewish war photographer who has been living for the past six months in Jerusalem with his documentary filmmaker wife and their three young children. He has already told me on the phone that he is desperate to show people the hidden side of Jerusalem. Drinking coffee near the Jaffa Gate, this deeply passionate, bright-eyed, playful man, who speaks French, Hebrew, English, Arabic and probably three other languages he doesn't use while we are together, tells me he is already known by the Israeli military as an 'Arab lover' and that he is deeply emotional about this conflict. He describes how he and his wife are documenting it up close.

'Are you ready to see it?' he asks. 'Ready to walk?'

We quickly move through the Christian quarter along the Via Dolorosa, held to be the path Jesus walked, carrying his cross, towards his crucifixion. Philip tells me of the Palestinian plight he has witnessed. Of his pain, his rage, his condemnation of Zionism. We huff and puff our way up the steep Mount of Olives as he explains about the settlements we pass.

We enter into the West Bank. He tells me the Israeli soldiers are watching us. I can see them above us in the gun turrets as we wander down the otherwise empty streets deeper into Palestine. Houses are literally split in half by the giant concrete slabs. We find many large, empty, rocket-propelled shells from a recent battle. We come to a spot where a lonely gas station sits next to the wall at a once-major intersection. When asked what he thinks about it, the station's owner tells us: 'This wall will come down. It took thirty years in Germany, and it's only been seven here so far.' He smiles.

We walk up to where an Israeli military group is stationed, protecting a large Jewish settlement. Banksy's street art plays with the other graffiti on the giant concrete wall. Exhausted, we take a Palestinian bus back to the old city, back through Lion's Gate, and eat hummus at the best hummus restaurant in the city. I tell Philip I want to stay in Israel a few days and then fly to Turkey. He says there is a better way.

'Through Jordan and Syria.'

Following Philip's itinerary a few days later, I'm out of the hostel with my ridiculously overpacked rolling backpack into the still boarded-up old city. It's early. I buy a Turkish coffee and some ring-shaped Arabic bread from a street vendor. I wait below the Golden Wall Hotel for the Palestinian shared taxi to Allenby Bridge – the crossing point from Palestine into Jordan. The plan is to get to Damascus, Syria, as quickly as possible, then hop the train to Aleppo, Syria, then cross through Turkey to Istanbul.

The small bus is full. We sit about an hour. Then we are all made to get off and buy tickets, during which process my window seat is taken. I'm now crammed in the back seat next to a ten-year-old who is eating a nasty-smelling meat pita of some kind. At first he won't sit next to me. Finally his mother makes him, as it is the only seat left. We drive into the West Bank and then through the desert, past camels, Bedouins driving herds of goats, lots of construction. It's a beautiful desert. Cream-colored. The little boy turns to me and says, 'I am clever. Are you clever?'

'I like to think I am. You speak good English,' I tell him.

'Thomas Edison was clever,' he says. We are friends now. The bus drives over the Jordan River and through the intense military check into Jordan. We get out to pay a hefty exit tax. The official asks for my visa.

'I've done lots of research and I'd like to buy one now,' I say.

'Not here you can't. You must go back to Jerusalem.'

I question this for a while only to learn that, well, yes, I can get a visa – but at the north crossing 130 kilometers away.

Through a quick, bizarre negotiation I pay a small fortune to a taxi dispatcher and I'm on the way. Back into Palestine and then into Israel. As I am with a Palestinian taxi, the security check and treatment by the Israeli military is heavy – seriously intimidating. They dismantle the taxi. Another hour and we get to the north crossing. I get out and walk to the crossing point; they glance at my passport and wave me through. No stamp. No questions. Nothing.

I'm in Jordan. That's it.

I say to the local bus manager that I want to go to the next border and cross into Syria.

'You have a visa?'

'No,' I tell him. 'They say I can get one at the border; it might take ten hours, but it can happen.'

'No, you go to Amman.'

After some haggling, a driver agrees to take me through Irbid to the Syrian boarder at Ramtha. On the way he tells me he lived in Texas for fifteen years and misses it so much he almost cries when he speaks of it.

'Texas is the land of freedom, real freedom, not like this place.' He gestures angrily out over the desert we drive through.

For the next hour he tells me about his wife, who was also his lawyer, and whom he refers to simply as 'bitch ... excuse me.' He explains that she had him kicked out of America, even though she is also Jordanian. As we drive, he gets a call, listens for a while and then turns to me: 'This is your lucky day. A guy I know knows the head guy at the Syrian boarder. He will drive you across, you pay him sixty dinars, he takes you through all the way to Damascus.'

One hundred bucks for a three-hour drive and a visa, sure ... We drive through Irbid, which, like all of Jordan, seems rough and tumble. He tells me proudly about the street here that has so many knit shops it is in the Guinness Book of Records. I like him. We pull over and I meet my mule into Syria. He is tough and doesn't speak English and seems a bit scared. They make sure I have taken out and destroyed any papers, currency or evidence that I have been in Israel. I was prepared for this from my research. I keep thinking how sad it is that the hatred between the Jews and Arabs is so strong that neither will allow visitors entry to their country if they have visited the other's country first.

'Do you have money to pay the police?'

'How much?'

'Just a few dinars.'

We go. The drive is fast and long to the boarder; the land seems meaner and more barren, the traffic more aggressive. We are waved through a crossing. I smile, and the driver gives me a 'not yet' motion. Another checkpoint. We pass easily through as he seems to know everyone.

Then we stop and enter a dirt-floored metal warehouse where a hundred or so men haggle in many lines. The sole female I see wears a burqua and full niqab so I cannot see her eyes. I am the only Westerner. For the first time, I feel real danger here. My guy runs around. I stand in line. He speaks to the customs officer: I'm stamped. We pass through another check and then another and I assume we are in Syria and I relax.

Then we pull up to a communist-style square structure. I follow him inside. This is Syrian customs. Big. Everything else to this point feels light. I see one long wall of glass with many lines of people. Behind the customs officers is a section of empty marble floor and, as if in a mirror, another group of officers with their backs to us and a wall of glass. We jockey for position in a few lines, my mule all over the place, and finally I'm in the diplomat-foreigners line. I give my passport to the big man in heavy uniform. A quick glance: 'No. No visa. Go back.'

My mule starts speaking rapidly.

The big man again: 'No. Go back. Wait five minutes.'

My mule runs off.

A group of young Chinese businessmen pushes ahead of me and gives the big man their passports.

'No. No visa. Go back.'

'But we are also socialist, we come from a socialist country,' one of the businessmen spurts to the big man in English.

'No, you go back. Wait five minutes. Sit.'

I wait. Again I approach the big man.

'Do you speak English?'

'Yes.'

'I'm told I can wait here, and then you can get me my visa for Syria, from here? I can wait, but is that true?'

'No, no visa. Go back. Wait five minutes.'

This is happening every few minutes to various people who approach, various groups. I am the only American. It feels like a game, so I wait, then a man quietly sitting in the corner says they haven't been giving Americans visas to Syria now for three months. I watch my guy running all around the intimidating building. He seems more and more agitated.

I approach the big man again, 'Okay, if no visa, can I have my passport back?'

'No, no visa. You go back. Wait five minutes.'

'I need my passport to go back.'

'You go back to Jordan.'

'I will, but I need my passport.'

'You wait.'

This goes on for another hour, my hopes up and down like a yo-yo, my heart pounding heavily now. Shit, what the fuck am I thinking trying to go to Syria? This is bad. I'm an American at the border between two nations that both hate America and they have taken my passport. No-one knows I'm here. How the fuck did losing a part in a Hollywood movie land me at a dangerous drug- and weapon-smuggling crossing into Syria?

Through the glass the big man stands and yells at me, 'You go to the other side and go!'

'I need my passport!'

'Other side.'

Now scared, I leave the building passport-less with my now crazed driver who hastily drives ahead to get yet another stamp on flimsy state paper at the next check. They reluctantly give him the stamped paper and we drive forward.

Very oddly I am in Syria.

Without a passport.

For a minute.

We turn around and go back, park, back inside, now on the other side of the mirror. They have no idea what I, or my driver, is talking about in either language. A Scandinavian man sits with all his packs on the floor. I get a bad vibe. He comes up and says he can't get his passport back unless he has a driver to Irbid. Can I take him? Fine, but I need my passport back first.

After much haggling and Kafkaesque behavior, an officer finally approaches the window with my passport. I reach in to grab it and he pulls it back just slightly. This is very subtle, but it goes on for five minutes, back and forth, always keeping my passport just slightly out of reach, my hand through the glass hole. He questions me, says okay, and again I try to take the passport and he pulls it back just slightly. Finally I and the bad-vibe Scandinavian are outside with our passports and luggage headed back to Jordan, and my driver, now deeply upset, wants to know how much I will pay him.

'Okay, look, I need to go to Amman now,' I say. 'You didn't get me to Damascus, so I'll give you the sixty dinars to get me to Amman now.'

The Scandinavian shrieks, 'Why are you overpaying him?'

'Look, man, I need to get back into Jordan, to Amman. I agreed to pay this guy; stay out of it.'

A wealthy-looking man approaches and becomes our translator, telling me that my mule says, 'No way, way too little money.' Now ignoring me, he then explains to my mule that the Scandinavian wants to go to Irbid.

'How much?'

'A few dinars,' spews the scrawny Scandinavian.

'No way.'

During all this I am also still haggling, only now to get to Amman. Finally the translator tells the Scandinavian it's twenty dinars to get to Irbid, at which he starts howling with scary manic laughter, spouting off about my overpaying the driver. He wanders away screaming, 'This is fucking crazy! Crazy! Crazy!'

We agree that I will go to Amman for a hundred dinars in total. I still haven't paid this guy a dime and it's been almost a full day and Amman is hours away. My translator explains that America stopped allowing Syrians with proper visas into the US and so this is their tit for tat. They officially say you can get in, get a visa, but you can't. There seems to be a lot of tit for tat in this part of the world. Karmically, 150 bucks for a full day of a taxi, a driver and all this madness doesn't feel so bad to me.

We head back into Jordan, through the first of the four checkpoints, where they now want to know where my Syrian stamp is. 'I didn't get one,' I explain. 'They wouldn't give me one.'

At each check my mule bribes and sweet-talks the customs officials. At one point things get heated and they physically take the taxi apart.

Finally we are back in Jordan. A mere hundred yards from the last checkpoint, we pull over and he passes me off to his son and his very rickety taxi, telling me in sign language that he is tired and the taxi we've been in all day isn't allowed into Amman. He wants the money. Uncomfortably I give in and give it to him and then his son asks over and over how to get to Amman. The old man, seemingly broken down by the day, relents and hands his son his keys and walks dejectedly to the smaller taxi. We are back together again. Through sign language he tells me he is sorry and that his friend at the Syrian border screwed him. He mock spits at him over and over. He seems sad, exhausted, very angry, embarrassed. I feel bad for him. He invites me to come to his home and eat and sleep and 'We go to Amman tomorrow?'

'I just can't do it,' I say.

He deflates and we begin the very long drive. After a few hours in the desert, we enter the sprawling city. Our drive through Amman to the airport takes about two hours. The nontourist version of the city is massive and rough, fires all over; a layer of smog and dirt make the sky dark. The place appears mean, forbidding, sad and endless. Most of the square concrete buildings seem to be missing many of their windows. Mix the worst part of industrial Queens and the area where they work on cars in Tijuana and that is what my two-hour drive through Amman offers. I don't see one green part, no trees, almost no color anywhere. Men share tea sitting in the middle of the road on mats using a kettle that looks like Aladdin's lamp.

Earlier the Scandinavian told me that he had been in Amman for two days and hated it and had to get out; he warned me to stay away. Finally, we are at the airport. I say goodbye to my mule, who seems relieved to have the whole ordeal over. We hug. I think in the end he was just an honest guy who was trying to make a buck but had a bad day due to his Syrian friend and sure didn't make much money for ten hours of driving, stress, haggling and actual danger attempting to bribe officials so as to get an American across one of the most nefarious border crossings on earth.

After a few hours of sleep at the awful Golden Tulip, the airport's only hotel, I'm back inside the airport. I haggle with a manager from Turkish Airlines to let me buy a ticket. The PA calls my flight to Istanbul. The Jordanian customs officer is very agitated. I don't have a stamp from Syria. Again the hatred of Israel. Lots of officials appear, military, they detain and question me for about a half hour. At one point I'm surrounded by cops, and officials, and officers all struggling to understand why I don't even have a piece of paper with a stamp from Syria. Finally after I basically beg them to let me just leave their country, they release me.

Sitting on the airplane flying to Istanbul, the woman sitting next to me tells me, 'Oh, Syria is magical.'

And I say with full sincerity, 'I was there once, but didn't get to see much.'

'Oh, you must go back!'

In this very moment sitting on the plane above Syria, I realize that I have my perspective back. That the bruises and cuts and mud covering my ego have disappeared and that the power and beauty of travel, even very challenging travel, have reconnected me to life.

Through Jordan and Syria and travel I have found my perspective. I can't wait to go back.

Discovering Armenia, Recovering Myself

ANDREA MARTIN

Andrea Martin is a mother of two fabulous sons, as well as a stage, television and film actress. She earned two Emmy Awards for writing on *Second City Television (SCTV)*, and has a Tony Award for Best Supporting Actress in the Broadway musical, *My Favorite Year*. She is also the recipient of three additional Tony Award nominations. Her film credits include *My Big Fat Greek Wedding,* for which she received a People's Choice Award for Best Ensemble. She has written and performed two one-woman shows, *Nude Nude Totally Nude* and *Andrea Martin: Final Days! Everything Must Go!!* She is currently writing a book for HarperCollins Canada.

For the longest time I wished I were Jewish. First of all, I looked the part. You know, big nose, dark eyes, pushy. Second of all, the Jews I hung out with – Mark Finks (my first boyfriend), Dr Alan Heifetz (my pediatrician) and Janet Shur (my superconfident best friend) – had a good time being Jewish. They owned who they were. They had so much self-esteem.

Unlike me. My parents – Sybil and John Martin – had gone to great lengths to assimilate and bury our ethnic identity, which was Armenian, distant cousin to Cher, Mike Connors, Charles Aznavour, and Clarabell the Clown. And you know who else? Arlene Francis from What's My Line? 'Is it larger than a breadbox? HAW HAW HAW.' My grandfather's name was Papazian, but when he came to the US in 1920, he saw the name 'Martin' on the side of a truck. So he took the name. He also took the truck.

As late as 1991, when I decided to write my first one-woman show, I didn't know where to find Armenia on a map. I thought it was a distant land that shipped frozen baklava to the corner deli. In fact, food was the only thing I associated with being Armenian. How was I going to write a one-woman show if I didn't know my roots? Who was this one woman who was about to reveal everything about herself? Up until that point, in my career, I had been playing characters, hiding in glasses, hats, wigs. Could I be on stage as myself without all my props and feel that I was enough? There was only one way to find out. I booked a flight to Armenia.

'Jesus Christ, Andrea! Why do you want to go there?' my father asked, as he grew more impatient and agitated by our conversation.

'Because I want to find out what it means to be Armenian, Daddy.'

'You won't find it out over there. The people are poor. The country is dirty. They have nothing.' He was getting angry. 'Besides, your family came from Turkey and they're all dead.'

Obviously, I knew nothing about my past. I went to the library and checked out everything ever written by, for and about Armenians. My dad was right. Historic Armenia was once a huge and prospering land that stretched between the Black Sea and the Caspian Sea to eastern Turkey. But all that remained of Armenia today, after years of invasions by the Romans, Persians, Arabs, Mongolians and Turks, was this small communist-ruled republic. Armenia: population 3 million. A tiny republic occupying 29,000 kilometers on the southwest tip of the Soviet Union. Surrounded by Georgia, Azerbaijan, Iran and Turkey.

But wait. It was the first nation in the world to adopt Christianity. That was impressive. I kept reading with growing awe and fascination. Armenia, where Noah landed his ark. Armenia, where the alphabet was invented. A proud race of survivors who had lived 3000 years. Survivor. I liked that word. It made me feel courageous. A brave crusader, right up there with Tigran the Great. Maybe I had been selected by some divine power to put Armenia back on the map. If Cher (Sarkisian!) wasn't going to jump on the bandwagon, then maybe I should. Fonda had Vietnam, Sting had the rain forest, but Armenia was still up for grabs. I closed my eyes. I saw my face on a stamp.

I prepared for my trip. I contacted Armenians who then gave me more names of Armenians to contact. Where had they been hiding all this time? Every Armenian I met wanted to help. I had more names that ended in 'ian' in my address book than were listed in Fresno's city directory. My bag was packed with 'souvenirs' I was told to bring. Bic lighters, bubblegum, decks of cards, costume jewelry, scarves, coffee, toilet paper, Handi Wipes, children's clothes, toys and eight-by-ten glossy pictures of myself. The last item was important, they said. 'You are a famous Armenian. People will be proud.'

By the time I boarded the plane, I looked like Margaret Mead about to document the aborigines. I was carrying a video recorder, a mini-cassette player, and a 35-millimeter camera. I was excited. I was hopeful. I knew that when my feet touched Armenian soil, I'd be home.

Here and now I would like to rewrite Thomas Wolfe: 'You can't go home a first time.' When my feet did touch land, nineteen hours later, all horrifyingly spent on the Devil's own airline, Aeroflot, I was just thankful to be alive. Flies buzzed inside the plane, pieces of ceiling dangled overhead, seat belts didn't fasten, and a stewardess slept throughout the trip. Just before we took off, two pilots staggered up and down the aisle. I was sure they were looking for the cockpit. But not one of the 300 Armenian passengers I was traveling with complained. In fact, they seemed happy. Men stood in aisles, chain-smoking, laughing. Women sat in heavy coats, guarding their bags. People sang. They were returning home to their loved ones. And I was an American girl, recording the event. I had never been around so many Armenians before. We had similar features, same color skin. But we seemed worlds apart.

It took four hours to get through customs. Armed Russian soldiers stood behind glass partitions. On the trip from the airport to the hotel, I saw lambs being slaughtered at the side of the road, barefoot children sleeping in makeshift houses, and decaying buildings left unfinished in hundred-degree heat. And everywhere I looked there were rocks. I knew that Armenia was called 'the land of stones,' and that only ten per cent of the country was covered by forests, but it seemed so barren and bleak. And backwards. Peasant women in shapeless, worn clothes sat on the ground selling yogurt and melons. Men pushed underfed cattle down the middle of the road. Traffic was at a standstill. And nothing seemed funny to me. A one-woman show? Every comedic bone in my body was broken. I didn't know what I had expected, but this certainly wasn't it. All my life I had felt like an outsider. Too ethnic for Maine. Too ethnic for Hollywood. And now I was too Waspy for Armenia. The Annette Bening of the Caucasus.

When we arrived in Yerevan, I clung desperately to my fading ideals. The city, one of the oldest in the world, seemed to be big and thriving and I'd always thought of myself as a big city girl. I hoped I might feel more at home. I got to the hotel and called some of the names on the lists I'd been given.

Greta, a fifty-year-old sister of a friend of a friend I had met in LA, was the first to arrive. She came with gifts of peaches and bread, and her dictionary, thank God. My only way of communicating was through mime. I'd spent a year studying with Jacques Lecoq in Paris, but aside from walking in place, I wasn't much good at making myself understood through visuals alone. Greta was unmarried, a physicist, and lived with her brother, his wife, their one-year-old child and her mother in a small walk-up flat in the city. She seemed so happy to see me. She hugged me and said, 'My English is poor, but I like very much to try.'

She apologized for not having a car. But there was a shortage of fuel and automobiles were scarce, she said. She then took me by the hand and escorted me through the city, all the while speaking slowly, and searching for words in her little book. 'You should see Armenia before the earthquake. Before the massacres in Baku and Karabakh. Here are many refugees. We are overcrowded. We live with blockades and corruption. Since *perestroika,* we don't know what to believe. And now you see, problems everywhere. But Armenia is beautiful county. You will find new energy here.' She showed me stone monuments of Armenian battles, bronze statues of Armenian heroes, and massive pink buildings made from tufa, the national stone. 'It is a wonderful rock,' she said proudly, 'our country's main source of wealth.'

I could see that the city had once been beautiful. But now in striking contrast to these magnificently crafted 'symbols' jutting into the sky were the shocking realities of Armenian everyday life. No food in the markets, just the occasional slab of fat in an unrefrigerated case. Empty cafés. No medicine. A few dreary, cheaply made clothes and shoes for sale. The opera, theater and museums were closed. 'It is too hot in August,' Greta said, 'to watch anything inside.' People stood idly on the streets, shaking their heads, many with blank stares. I recognized the faces. They looked no different from the faces of my ancestors, who had fled their homeland 100 years ago. Little had changed. There were few tangible reminders of a flourishing civilization that once had given birth to the most distinguished artists, musicians and intellectuals in the world. How could anyone live here, I thought. Life seemed so impossible.

For the next ten days I submerged myself in the country. Armenians gave me food when they didn't have any, drove me in cars that they had to borrow. Everyone welcomed me. They showed me how proud they were to be Armenian and how important it was for me to feel that way too. I was shown ancient pagan temples, monasteries from the twelfth century, and churches hand-carved out of stone. There were 4000 churches still standing in Armenia today, I was told. I was overwhelmed by each Armenian's knowledge of their history, and grateful and exhausted by their hospitality. 'I want to be alone,' I soon found out, was not part of the Armenian vocabulary.

We spent evenings talking and philosophizing about the Turks, communism, seventy years of an evil regime, and the future of the country. They wanted an independent Armenia, and were fighting for it. The newly elected President was on their side. It might take years. But they were prepared. They had no other choice.

I grew to love these people and their undying spirit. And I began to find my humor again, and to understand theirs. 'Do you know what makes an Armenian laugh?' Samvel Shahinian asked me during a dinner he had prepared for me one night. He was an artist and theoretician, and his beautiful and gracious wife, Gulnara, was the director of Foreign Affairs in Yerevan.

'What?' I asked, hoping that the door to our mutual comedy psyches might finally be unlocked. He held his hand up, and moved his little finger back and forth. I laughed.

'See?' he said. 'Anything.'

I asked him how Armenians could find humor in the terrible conditions in which they were forced to live and he replied, 'Because, you see, things cannot get much worse.' I began to see, in each and every Armenian, courage, the kind of courage I had never known, that despite the terrible hardships and living conditions, they still woke up with their dreams. I asked why they didn't leave and come to America, where they could have a better life. And they answered simply, with a quiet dignity and resolve, 'If we go, there will be no Armenia.'

I thought about how safe and connected I felt surrounded by people who shared my history, whose ancestors were mine. I saw my grandmother's face. When I was growing up, Nanny lived with us in a room next to mine, a room she rarely left. She'd sit for hours, crocheting and staring out the window. I suppose she was remembering, but she never spoke of her past. My mother told me that Nanny had been brought to

America when she was fifteen, in an arranged marriage, and had had five children with a man twenty years older, a man she never loved. She had lost her father and brothers in the Armenian Genocide, and had to leave her mother behind. She could never return to her homeland. I remember wanting to make Nanny happy, to hug her and make all her pain go away. But I couldn't. I was a child and I didn't understand. So I ran from her sadness. I couldn't even look at the sadness in myself. Turned it into a career of comedy. Kept it as far away as I could. I cut off my roots before they even had a chance to grow.

By the time my trip ended, I was anxious to get home. I missed my kids. All lines to the US had been cut off for a week. I wanted to take a shower. I wanted to sleep in a rodent-free room. I also wanted a real cup of coffee. Armenia received its coffee from Russia, caffeine-free. The government, I was told, controlled all 'drugs.'

Greta and her brother drove me to the airport. We were silent all the way. As we stood outside customs, Armenians pushed and yelled and crammed their way past us. Greta apologized for their behavior. 'They are animals,' she explained, 'because no-one has come to show them how to do better.' Self-reliance had to be taught to Armenians again. Everyone knew this. I wanted to believe that nothing could destroy our race. If we had survived 3000 years, I hoped we could survive 3000 more. I hugged Greta. There were tears in our eyes.

On August 16, 1991, I returned to Los Angeles, one day before the Soviet coup. I feel privileged that I was in Armenia while the next chapter in their history was being written. After seventy years of Soviet rule, they were finally on their way to freedom.

I opened my one-woman show *Nude Nude Totally Nude* at the Joseph Papp Public Theater on April 6, 1996. There were many laughs in the show. But for the first time in my life I dared to not get laughs. It took courage. Not the courage of Tigran the Great, but in my own way, I was defending my people by just getting up there. In my own way, I was preserving my culture, like my boyfriend Mark Finks had preserved his. There may not have been many Armenians in the audience, but getting onto that stage, I was surrounded by 3000 years of history – like an actor playing Lear for the first time, who is never alone but embraced by all those who played the part before him. Finally, I belonged. The part of me I'd cut off, I'd found.

I was enough.

Arctic Adventure

BROOKE SHIELDS

An accomplished model, author and television, film and theater actress, Brooke Shields began her career at the age of nine. Her acting credits include the films *Pretty Baby*, *The Blue Lagoon* and *Endless Love*, and the TV shows *Suddenly Susan*, *That '70s Show* and *Lipstick Jungle*. She is the author of the *New York Times* bestseller *Down Came the Rain: My Journey Through Postpartum Depression*, and the children's books *Welcome To Your World, Baby* and *It's the Best Day Ever, Dad!* She received a degree in French literature from Princeton University, graduating with honors. She currently lives on the East Coast with her husband and two daughters.

Several years ago, I got a call about contributing to *Marie Claire* magazine as a writer. The series of articles they were doing entailed engaging various actresses to go on trips and document their experiences.

Marie Claire chose the locations and matched them with the actresses. They had sent Demi Moore to be alone for a three-day yoga retreat in the mountains of Idaho during the summer. They had sent Gwyneth Paltrow to a deserted, tropical island for three days of solitude. The magazine explained that the article was to document the unique experience the actress was being subjected to. After hearing the locations they had chosen for the other two, I thought, 'Sure, I could handle some R&R.' I was positive I would be sent to some warm, mystical place where I would eat berries and watch multicolored sunsets.

Eager to hear my particular assignment, I called the magazine and said, 'Yes, I'd love to go on a trip for you and write about it. Where are you going to send me?'

The answer was chilling: 'We want you to go to the Arctic and build an igloo by yourself and sleep in it overnight!'

Great, I thought. Send the big girl to the Arctic while the petite ones get warm weather and sand! But never having been a person to back out of a commitment, and buoyed by the prospect of seeing the northern lights, I said, 'I can't wait.'

My best friend had just died suddenly and I had been devastated by the loss. I needed to escape my life in any way possible. I wanted to go someplace where I could be under the radar and have time to think and mourn. Well, I was about to get my chance to do just that and maybe even get a glimpse of the northern lights. Even though it would be the opposite of warm weather and tropical sunsets, I was game for the adventure. And what an adventure it would turn out to be!

We left LA – where it was seventy degrees and sunny – with a suitcase filled with North Face snow gear and flew all night to Ottawa, Canada. We then boarded a jet that was half used for cargo and half for passengers for a three-hour ride involving multiple stops. As the terrain below changed from green and hilly to gray and mountainous and then white and jagged, I began to wonder if I had made a mistake. The farther we traveled, the more unforgiving the land became.

When we arrived in Iqaluit, the temperature was twelve degrees below zero and dropping. At this particular time of the year, we were told, there would be only two hours a day of minimal daylight. When I heard this, I actually started to worry that I'd get depressed by the lack of light. My husband and I were dating at the time and he had agreed to be my travel companion; he told me to calm down and embrace the experience.

Within thirty-nine seconds of deplaning, I had no feeling in my fingers or toes, my digital camera had seized up, my nose hairs had frozen, and I could not take in a deep breath. The pilots informed us it would drop to thirty below within the next few hours. We were in for it and I had to rally emotionally. I decided to push away fears of the cold and of getting SAD – seasonal affective disorder – and turned to Chris and said, 'Here we go, babe. We will laugh about it all one day.'

Our first stop was the equipment store, where we were outfitted with caribou skins, seal boots and gloves. For years the Inuit have perfected the art of survival by using only the resources available to them. Whenever we stopped to talk to the Inuit and told them I was to build an igloo, two traditions always came up: boot chewing and wife swapping. To soften their men's boots, we were told, the women chew on the leather, gnawing at it until it is soft and pliable. Second, if an Inuit seeks refuge in your igloo, it is customary to offer food, shelter and your wife! I whispered to Chris that neither of the two traditions would happen as long as I was 'his woman!'

We spent our first night in a hotel to acclimatize. I stared hard out the window but saw no northern lights.

The next morning we flew up the coast in a small plane, making three stops along the way to pick up various biologists, caribou researchers and a stray, injured hunter in need of medical attention twelve hours away. Did I mention that medical attention was twelve hours away?

We landed in Pond Inlet, probably one of the northernmost inhabited towns on the continent. My eyelids froze and we were 400 miles into the Arctic Circle! And this was a good idea, why?

The next stop was at a private home to spend the night. The family could not have been sweeter and they had a meal ready for us. At one point the guide (I use that term lightly), 'Hammy,' asked if I would like to go outside and get some ice for our drinks. I thought it was strange that they did not have ice-cube trays in the freezer. It turned out that you had to go into the backyard and use a pick to get chunks of ice off a huge iceberg that had been trapped in the frozen sea. It would sit there until summer, when it would continue its migration south. For the time being, it served as the world's largest ice cube.

The first thing I saw out back was a dead seal on the ground. I gasped and it was quickly explained to me that Inuit eat seal meat and that their size prohibits them from fitting in the freezer. Basically, the whole backyard was a freezer. My eyes adjusted and I looked up and saw something out of the original *Frankenstein* movie. It was an enormous mountain of ice. I was in awe of its magnitude and could not stop myself from sprinting towards it. I had never seen anything so massive and ominous. But as big as it was, it felt quiet.

It was dark outside, but the moon provided a faint, beautiful hue. As I ran up to the ice to place my hands on it, I suddenly heard Hammy screaming at me. I looked back and saw him running towards me clutching a long metal pole (which he later referred to as a 'hunter's friend').

My mind raced. Fearing I had done something against the Inuit gods or that there was a massive animal about to devour me, I held my hands in the air as if being arrested. As he reached me and started yelling in a mix of English and Yupik, the tabloid headline flashed through my brain: 'American Actress Stabbed in Heart by Rabid Inuit Guide.'

Hammy quickly showed me that if I had gone one step further, I would have fallen into a space that ran around the circumference of the iceberg. Evidently icebergs occasionally shift. The slightest movement from such a huge object breaks the ice that surrounds it. People sometimes fall between the gap and can die.

Shaken, but alive, I stood still and did what he told me. He showed me with his spear that the water was beyond deep. He then picked off a chunk of ice to bring back to the house. He went ahead and motioned for me to follow.

I did but then stopped, turning back for a moment to take it all in.

I stood alone and silent, in the faint moonlight. I fell to my knees to reflect. In front of me stood this monumental, peaceful, yet powerful, monolith, and beneath me the ice contained a turbulent sea. Even though there were still no northern lights to see, I felt a part of something glorious and big. I wanted to honor the moment, so I said a prayer for my deceased friend and for peace of mind and heart for myself and for those in need. Somehow I felt my friend was looking after me and figured he did not want me joining him anytime soon!

Once back in the house I got a good look at the chunk of ice. I had never seen a more beautiful blue. It actually glowed. And the taste was the most refreshing clean taste I had ever experienced. Ice! Who knew it could evoke such emotion?

After dinner we all went to sleep. It had been a long day and we were beginning at five o'clock the next morning. At bedtime it was actually lighter than when we awoke five hours later.

The next part of our journey involved breaking in a new sled dog. This sounded like fun. We met the team of dogs, who were eager to begin their run. I asked if I could pet them and was told it was fine. I was informed, however, that the dogs were not considered pets, but were basically 'employees.' The owners of the teams rarely caressed them but instead fed them raw meat and taught them to run. I went up to a huge malamute and kneeled down in from of him so as to seem less like an alpha or a threat. The dog started to whimper in a happy way and began to lick my face and wiggle. I almost cried. I did not, but little did I know that the tears would come soon enough.

The next step was to harness up the team, including the new pup. This was a trip designed to see if the rookie dog could handle being a sled dog. I jumped on the sled in my enormous caribou suit and held on for dear life. The guide cracked the reins and off we went into a vast, white-covered abyss.

Within seconds the newbie pub was squealing and flopping around like a fish out of water. At one point he went under the blades of the sled. I became Marilyn Monroe in *The Misfits,* screaming and crying and trying to jump off the sled to rescue the dog. The guide held me back and then in a flash had cut the dog free from the tangled mess. He cut him loose with a knife and left him in the snow.

I was sobbing but we continued on for a two-hour ride. I had been a witness to Darwin's theory of 'survival of the fittest' and was not happy about it. I later learned that the dog was fine but that if he could not hack it, he just would not make the team. Taking him back to New York City was not an option, as Chris quickly made clear. Maybe he could become a pet after all?

The rest of that day was spent meeting different people of the town and visiting the post exchange and the local museum filled with the most beautiful artifacts and traditional clothing from preceding Inuit generations. We were told that for the Inuit people, meals usually consisted solely of caribou meat and Arctic char. I was just so thankful that seal was not on the menu. It is almost impossible to get vegetables or fruit flown in to Iqaluit, so their diet is quite limited but unbelievably low in fat. However, because of the post exchange, they are now seeing a rise in obesity and heart disease. The younger generations were trading in the fat-free diet for pizza, Philly cheese steaks and fried food.

That night we left our hosts' home and drove way out to a tiny hotel in the middle of nowhere for the night. There we would sleep and trade in our fur suits for our heavy-duty snow gear. By this time I had no idea what time of day it was or what to feel. I hardly slept in anticipation of my task of building an igloo and sleeping in it.

Within a few hours we were all up drinking instant coffee and being led to the igloo site.

When we trekked to the site, 'Hammy' had already built a beautiful igloo as a reference and started the task of teaching me how to build one: draw a circle in the snow about twelve feet in diameter. Then, using a saw (originally they used a whalebone), cut rectangular blocks of ice. Each block was knee high, four inches deep and the width of a typical doorway.

The assignment was that I do it alone. I started to saw away and after two hours almost passed out with fatigue. I stacked the blocks around the circle I had drawn. Once I had ten more blocks I started stacking them around myself. I continued with the process, each level tilting and spiraling toward the sky above, corners pressing against each other for support. I kept looking over at the completed and perfect igloo and almost cried.

At the top I was supposed to leave a small gap for air. Hammy helped me put on the final block and then cut out my door. After about three hours, I filled the cracks with snow and stared with pride at my successfully constructed, slightly lopsided, Picasso-esque, but functional, igloo.

We took a break and I posed for some photos inside Hammy's perfect igloo. A lamp had been put in its center on the ground, and from the outside the igloo glowed beautifully. It was perfect for a photo. The guide went in to man the lamp. I crawled in with him to stick my head out for a photo. Suddenly I smelled kerosene and Hammy, once again, was yelling at me!

But this time it was to run, not stop running. The stove had been given too much gas and had caught fire. Flames were leaping up and blanketing the ceiling, charring the entire inside of the igloo. I scrambled out of the small entrance and ran as fast as my frozen legs would go. Chris later recalled the humor of seeing such a sight. One minute I was smiling for a photo, the next I was screaming and running like a crazy lady with a burning stove flying through the air after me. Once again I had narrowly escaped injury and possible death. And once again I pictured Demi and Gwyneth saying 'Om' and finding inner peace!

I really wanted to laugh when I saw that Hammy had burned the tip of his nose, but he was already embarrassed and my cheeks were too frozen to move.

When it was dinnertime at my igloo, I served – can you guess? – Arctic char and caribou, but added some garlic I had bought in town. You had to eat it fast because it got cold from the pan to your mouth and froze before you could clean your plate.

The time had come to sleep in my masterpiece. Chris and I got out sleeping bags and caribou pelts and some whiskey and proceeded to become situated. The best way to sleep in eight-degree weather is to strip down to fleece, get in your sleeping bag and kick your feet around. The idea is to heat the immediate area around you. I thought that whiskey and fatigue would aid in my sleeping. What I did not know was that I had acute claustrophobia.

The moment I got in the bag and got horizontal, my chest tightened and I started to panic and hyperventilate. It was thirty degrees below zero outside, so leaping out of the igloo in my underwear was not an option. Chris did not slap me or yell 'Snap out of it!' like in the movie *Moonstruck,* but he suddenly grabbed my face and made me look into his eyes and listen as he talked. He explained how I was not stuck. I could open the little door and walk away. There was land for miles and I could run on it. After a while of saying prayers and repeating 'I am fine' as a mantra, I fell asleep.

I slept soundly until about 6am when I felt Chris's hands vigorously brushing at my face. Instead of the calm eyes I had looked into not hours before, this time his face showed signs of dread. Apparently because I was too claustrophobic to cover my face with my sleeping bag, condensation had frozen on my cheeks. To him I looked dead! He laughed with relief when I asked, 'What on earth are you doing?'

A slight glow of the early morning was beginning to creep through the hole at the top of my igloo. I sighed with relief knowing that my task was completed. I had done it. I had survived. I had built an igloo and we had spent the night outside in the Arctic. Mission accomplished! Take that, warm, bikini-clad ladies!

It was time to leave. We all gathered and took a plane to Iqaluit, where we were introduced to an elderly Inuit grandmother who wanted to give us a proper Inuit farewell ceremony. She lit a traditional stove made out of soapstone (one that would not blow up!). As she looked at the flame, she sang an ancient Inuit song for us. Her voice was haunting. The song was about being young and going out on your first hunt.

Somehow, I identified with that song. In many ways a new chapter of life was beginning for me, and I had also just gone through an experience reminiscent of a rite of passage. I had begun my mission with some trepidation but I was leaving Iqaluit stronger and more confident. We thanked her and said our many goodbyes.

As I was about to board the plane the grandmother grabbed my arm and pointed up above. Wafting through the dark afternoon sky was a luminescent cloud, a gentle radiance: the northern lights. We all stood silently and offered our own individual prayers into the universe. Even though I was not on a beach or in any sunlight, I had experienced more warmth than I could ever have imagined. The Inuit people had opened up their hearts and homes to us. And the universe had whispered, 'It is all going to be okay.'

Non Mia Piace Siena

EILEEN HEISLER

Eileen Heisler has enjoyed a twenty-year career writing television comedy, currently as co-creator and executive producer of the hit series *The Middle*, starring Patricia Heaton. Born and raised in the suburbs of Chicago, she lives in Pacific Palisades, California, with her husband, Adam Wolman, and nonidentical twin boys, Justin and Ben (age twelve). This is her first foray into travel writing.

Non mia piace Siena.
I don't like Siena. Sorry, I just don't.

I know I should. They say it's lovely. They say it's a second Florence.

I wouldn't know.

It started with a circle. A road sign with a circle, and an arrow in the center that said *'Centro'* – or maybe it was a dot … I don't remember exactly, but as I clutched the wheel of the only automatic rental car in Italy – twenty-six years old, with my 24-year-old sister by my side and our overstuffed backpacks in the backseat – I saw a simple sign with a circle and a dot: *centro*. Center … the center of the city – and all roads lead to it. Easy. Simple …

Wrong.

Sweat beading on my lip, heart pounding, how long had we been driving? I was losing track of time. All these signs … promising me a *centro* that I wasn't finding. Marcy made suggestions: 'Haven't we gone this way already?' I don't know! I was older, I was in charge, and we were driving in circles … lost. Just the same damn sign, *Centro,* I get it I get it. But where?

Forget it. This wasn't working in a car. We needed to ditch the car and start walking. We just had to find a parking garage, but the signs to the garage were as useless as the signs to the *centro*. We had to get out of this car! Oh, is that a space? Seems legal. Let's just get out and we'll walk to the *centro*. But how would we remember where we parked? We looked around for a touchstone. We were right next to an Esso gas station and an Api gas station. Perfect.

We locked the car, heaved a sigh of relief, grabbed our guidebooks, strapped on our fanny packs, and set out to find our way. And there, lo and behold, a sign with a circle, *'Centro.'* That way. We'd had no luck in the car, but maybe if we just trusted our feet ... The air felt cool on our faces. Now we could think clearly. Now we were out of the car. Now we would find the *centro*.

We walked, following crowds down the winding medieval roads. In the *centro* would be the square, we could navigate back from there. Once we found it.

But we didn't.

Was it the driving that had unmoored us? Where was our sense of direction? I was hungry, dizzy ... Whose idea was it to make a circular city, anyway? We had been lost for about four hours. Lost in a car, now lost on foot ...

My little sister was starting to doubt me. I could feel it. Well, maybe not starting to doubt me. Probably started doubting me a week earlier when, as we were getting off the plane, I suddenly blurted to a flight attendant, *'Non parlo inglese!'* I don't speak English. Idiot. So, yeah, my leadership abilities as the chief navigator through Europe were probably not very confidence inducing.

Well, we walked and walked ... and eventually we reached a square. Was this the *'centro'* we had been promised? Couldn't tell. It seemed central. There were restaurants.

At last, we dropped, exhausted, into café chairs. We sat and ate – I'm guessing I had gnocchi. I think I had gnocchi everywhere. It was a word I knew. At this point in the trip I felt fairly confident that gnocchi and wine was a meal I could order in Italian without too much embarrassment. So we ate gnocchi, and we caught our breath, and we laughed over the adventure of the day and the fact that we'd spent so much time lost that eating this meal was probably the only thing we'd do in Siena.

No time for museums, no time for sights. Who could find them? In that moment we were not lost. We were in a square in Siena and all was well.

For that moment.

Hours later. We're lost, Leeny! We're lost. This isn't the way. We'll never get out! Fine! You find it, then. I'm not Italian, I've never been here before. Why the hell are you following me, anyway? I don't know where I'm going, I don't know! We walked, and we bickered – two short, curly-haired exhausted girls from the suburbs, fighting our way through the crazy rat-maze that is Siena, bickering and fighting and bickering and fighting our way out ... to the car. That was parked near a Benetton on the outskirts of the city ... between an Esso station and an Api station ...

That was nowhere to be found.

And then reality hit me. Lost in a car, lost on foot, and now... lost the car? The car with all our stuff in it that was parked somewhere outside this circular city and we had no idea where it was. Tears welled up in our eyes. Which of us was going to admit we were seriously fucked? Everything looked familiar, nothing looked familiar ... Marcy looked at me, shook her head and wailed, '*Non mia piace Siena.*' No, I said. Me neither.

And then I actually began running scenarios through my head. What if we never found the car? Could we just ditch it, and all our stuff inside, hop a train for somewhere and hope for the best. Did we need stuff? Did we need anything? 'Cause we were never gonna find the car.

Turns out Esso stations and Api stations are pretty common sights in Italian cities ... there are hundreds of 'em.

So we looked at each other, and we knew what we had to do. Here in this ancient city we would turn to the wisdom of the ages – we would call upon everything we'd ever learned at Eileen Boevers Performing Arts Workshop, taught in a garage in Highland Park, Illinois – improv ... drama ... expressive dance.

And so we started yelling, desperate, to every passerby, arms waving, faces contorted – 'Esso, Api?' 'Esso, Api?!' Miming and gesticulating to show that these two landmarks were side by side. 'Esso, Api?' *Pierdo el automovil* (complete with gestures of driving and shrugging). 'We lost our car!!!' Esso, Api? Esso, Api? Old, young, the citizens of Siena nodded politely, they smiled, not understanding. One man gestured to the sky and mimed an umbrella, *'Piogga,'* he said. Yes, sir. *Piogga.* It is, indeed, starting to rain.

We walked, and we ran, and we got wetter, our hair flattened to our heads, as our pantomime, dance, dramatic international improv plea grew more frantic, more urgent, with each passing hour ... the light dimming, the sun setting, Esso, Api? Esso, Api?!

And then an old man in a gray coat nodded. Esso, Api. And pointed. Over there.

We looked at him in disbelief, and then in the direction he was pointing. And there, like a vision ... an Esso station. An Api station right next to it. A Benetton nearby. And in front. All by itself. Our car.

Esso, Api! Esso, Api! We flung our arms around him in joy, as he nodded politely and a little confused at our sudden outpouring of affection. And still shouting 'Esso, Api' we waved a grateful goodbye to the glorious man in the gray coat – the glorious man who understood. And we ran toward the car, and collapsed, in relief, across its hood. Esso, Api. Yes.

If you keep following a circle, you will get back to where you started. And as I looked at my sister, her head thrown back, curls flying, familiar twinkle in her blue eyes, flopped over the car in grateful desperation as we laughed and laughed over our absurdity ... I knew I had. In a foreign country, all grown now, living on separate coasts, we were, nonetheless, back where we started. My sister and me. *Il centro*. The dot at the center of who we are. Or was it an arrow? I can't remember.

Mia piace me sorella. Mia piace l'Italia.

But *non mia piace Siena*. Sorry. I just don't.

Miami Diary

ROLF DE HEER

Rolf de Heer writes, produces and directs feature films. Works include *Ten Canoes, The Tracker* and *Bad Boy Bubby. The Old Man Who Read Love Stories,* of which this is just one such story, was filmed in 1999 in French Guyana, after actor kidnap insurance was unobtainable for shooting in Venezuela or Colombia.

I'm staying at a hotel in Miami. Not just any hotel, but Loews Miami Beach Hotel. The hotel Richard Dreyfuss is staying in. Not the worst hotel I've ever stayed in (that's still reserved for the best hotel in Puerto Ayacucho) but the hotel I hate more than any hotel I've ever stayed in.

Figure it this way. Friday morning I'm in the jungle ... deep in the jungle in French Guyana, staying in a place where they can't have small animals as pets because they attract jaguars. The nearest settlement is an hour away by boat. The jungle is thick, peaceful, magnificent.

It's still early morning when I walk towards the boat to leave; mist still hangs in the treetops. I take the long trip by boat, my ass still sore from the epic boat journey the previous day. I arrive at the settlement and walk up the hill and through town. By now it's hot and I sweat freely. Eventually I get to the place where the 'taxi' is meant to pick me up (apart from tractors, there appear to be only two vehicles in this town, both vans, which are used to ferry things and people between town and the airport). The taxi arrives; I journey the slow and extremely bumpy journey to the airport. I wait.

Eventually the twenty-seater arrives. Twenty passengers and too much hand luggage are crammed into the little fuselage. The plane stands on the dirt tarmac, baking. The twenty passengers sit inside, being baked, the air almost unbreathable. A tropical storm passes, the plane starts up and we're off. The air begins to move, inside the plane and out.

It's the air moving outside that's the trouble. It's moving rather too much for my (and everybody else's) liking. The little plane is thrown around in the air like a leaf. People scream. Others are silenced. Some are crying.

We make it to Cayenne. I find the rest of my luggage, most of which has been left in Cayenne, and gratefully put on a pair of dry socks and shoes; by now I'm a little sick of wearing wet socks and wet boots. I wait for the flight to Miami.

Eventually I'm allowed to stop waiting and I board the plane … one class only. I'm wedged in the middle seat, between a thin six-foot-eight German scientist whose legs must encroach on my territory (nowhere else for them to go) and a fat man of uncertain nationality whose arm must encroach on my territory (nowhere else for it to go).

We take off. Again it's a pretty wild ride, again there are screams, but this is a much bigger plane and eventually it finds its way over and around the storms. We're fed (sort of). The journey goes on. And on.

Suddenly we land somewhere, I don't know where. I'm dying for a cigarette, and to buy something English to read I've read Wednesday's copy of the *Herald Tribune* twice, including the financial pages and the stock exchange reports. But we're not allowed to get off the plane.

The plane swelters on the tarmac and now some people do get off. Unfortunately, neither the scientist nor the fat man does. I stay wedged, no room to work, nothing to read. Some people get on, then there's an argument about seats. There are no facilities for seat allocation at this airport, so all the newcomers sit just anywhere, but there are too many people and not enough seats. Babies are crying.

The flight crew have got lists, so they start to allocate seats. The culprits are found, a couple of blokes attempting to get through to Miami by staying on the plane. The plane takes off without them and I wonder what's to become of them.

Within twenty minutes we land again ... somewhere else or the same place? There's confusion about getting off or staying on. I decide I've heard we're allowed to get off if we want to, so I do, not caring much if the plane takes off without me. There's a terminal, modern, with shops, but smoking is forbidden. I prowl the bookshop for something in English. There are hundreds of magazines, thousands of books, dozens of newspapers, but everything's in French or Spanish, even the girlie magazines. The only English publication is a *Hot Rod* magazine. I'm not so desperate.

I notice a huddle of uniforms, flight attendants and pilots. French. Hah, where there's an accumulation of French people, there must be smoking. It's true ... the outer ring of nonsmokers is protecting the inner ring of smokers from sight. Such loyalty and devotion to one's fellow workers. I pretend, in my Balinese shirt and Akubra hat, to be a French flight attendant. They understand. I'm accepted as one of them, even by the nonsmokers. And they say the French are arrogant.

There is movement, we get back on the plane. We must get back into our allocated seats, even though minutes later the free-for-all scramble of the new passengers happens again. We take off again ... two hours to Miami!

I'm wrong. Two-and-a-half hours to Haiti, no reading, no video, no room to sleep. We land in Haiti, the runway feels like it needs repairing.

This time we must get off the plane. We're locked into a large room ... too many people, air-conditioning doesn't work, thoughts of the Black Hole of Calcutta. No shops, no smoking, not much fun. People complain, nothing can be done. I'm tired, nothing can be done.

Back on the plane again ... two hours to Miami! I was in the jungle this morning ...

>>>>>>>>>>>>>>>

Miami Diary

At Miami someone opens an overhead locker and my computer falls out, landing on someone else's head and then straight to the floor. It's picked up and thrown onto a seat. The fat man has decided there's no reason to rush, so he waits for most of the passengers to be off the plane before he moves and the scientist and I can straighten our legs. This patience turns out to be a mistake. Most of the people on the flight are unable to fill in their customs or immigration forms correctly. The customs and immigration people are remarkably good-humored and friendly about this. I guess it helps that most of them are black, as are the incoming illiterates. The queue moves very slowly.

I'm through and collect my bag. Even though I look suspiciously like a drug dealer, I'm allowed through without a search ... maybe I look too obvious. By now it's ten o'clock at night, and the mist in the treetops was a long time ago. I stagger out of the terminal into an oven of exhaust fumes and noise. I light up a cigarette and add to the pollution.

Seconds later a taxi stops in front of me, the driver gesturing that I should get in. I gesture back, indicating I want to have my cigarette in peace. He opens the window and yells at me, I can have my cigarette in the taxi. He's so urgent about it, so worried about getting caught for jumping the queue, that I think fuck it and throw my bags into the taxi and clamber in after.

He opens all the windows to dissipate the cigarette smoke and begins, in very bad English, to explain that his father smokes – unbelievable, unbelievable! A packet a day! Unbelievable! Smokes while he's eating his soup because it tastes better! Unbelievable!

Then more unbelievable! Which would I take, a million dollars or one cent doubled each day for thirty days? I rather spoil his excitement by saying I'd take the one cent. I ask him where he's from; he says Colombia. I ask him how long he's been here; he says, all his life, he was born in Miami. Unbelievable, he says, everybody wants the million dollars. I do a quick calculation and say I'd end up with $15 or $16 million in the thirty days. Unbelievable, he says.

We get to the hotel, but not before he manages to tell me the cheapest rooms are more than $500 a night (this turns out to be untrue). Unbelievable, I say. The fare is twenty-five dollars. I hand him a fifty and ask for a receipt. He gives me a receipt but no change, and starts to take off while I'm still half in the cab. I yell and he stops. I retrieve my change and give him five bucks. You never know with Colombians, even those born in Miami.

I enter the hotel lobby, and none of my experiences of the previous sixteen hours has prepared me for the assault on my senses. They don't play muzak in the lobby, but the local FM station is blasted out at full volume. There's a band playing at the other end; the two musics fight. The air-conditioning is on so high that within minutes I'm shivering. People walk around yelling into mobile phones. Americans walk around yelling at hotel staff. People at the front desk put on a brave face, but they've been yelled at by Americans all day and at best the service is perfunctory.

I'm booked into a nonsmoking room. I ask for a smoking room but they say they haven't got any. I don't believe them but I don't want to start behaving like an American. Where can I smoke then? In the lobby or outside. In the lobby it's minus degrees and neo-Breughel with contemporary noise. Outside it's still ninety-five degrees (really) and exhaust fumes. This morning I was in the jungle.

I last half a cigarette in the lobby, then go to my room where at least it's quiet. I turn off the air-conditioner and try to open the windows ... no luck there, the building is almost hermetically sealed.

Miami Diary

I decide to go to sleep. The room is too stuffy without air-con, so on goes the air-con and on come the blankets. (There's a lunacy about having to have two blankets when the temperature outside is still ninety-two degrees at midnight, but that's America.)

I wake up early, eye the minibar but resist, going downstairs instead. 'Where do I go to have breakfast?' I ask the front desk clerk. 'Depends what you want,' he says. 'Breakfast is included in my booking,' I explain. He peers at the computer screen ... 'It's not,' he says.

'It may not be on your computer,' I counter, 'but that doesn't mean it hasn't been paid for. It simply means it isn't on your computer.' I try to stay very nice, very un-American. I volunteer to go upstairs and get the booking confirmation. I come back with it.

'I was afraid I'd be wrong,' he says, and hands me three breakfast vouchers.

'Where do I go with these?' He points to a sort of stall in the middle of the lobby, selling coffee and pastries. I wander over to the stall. I'm told I'm allowed a juice, a pastry and a coffee. I select a mango juice and a pastry and ask for a caffe latte (they have a machine!).

'That'll be seven dollars.' I look strangely at the attendant. I had just handed her a breakfast voucher. She looks strangely at me: 'You're only allowed orange juice and American coffee.' What an idiot I am.

She hands me the orange juice and the American coffee in polystyrene mugs, the pastry on a polystyrene plate with a plastic knife. 'Sugar's over there.' I get a little bag of sugar and sit down in the cold, with some contempo rock star blaring out at six in the morning. I drink the juice. Almost cool. I take a bite of the pastry. Sort of fresh. I pour the little bag of sugar into the coffee ... nothing to stir it with.

I go back to the stall and look around for a teaspoon. I can't see any. 'What do you want now?' she says.

'A teaspoon, please.'

She looks at me strangely. 'A what?'

'A teaspoon.'

She can't figure this out, looks at me even more strangely. 'You know, to stir the sugar into my coffee.'

She points vaguely to a beaker with clear plastic drinking straws in it. 'There.'

I tentatively take a straw. 'One of these?'

She looks at me as if I'm completely gone and nods.

I take the drinking straw back to my little part of Alaska and stir my coffee. One sip confirms its undrinkability. I go back to the stall to order a proper coffee, to hell with the expense. She sees me coming and quickly turns her back and pretends to be busy, hoping I'll go away. I'm patient. She can't keep it up for very long, there's no-one else in the lobby at that time of morning.

'Yes?'

'I'd like a caffe latte please.'

'It'll cost you ... '

'That's all right. Better to pay for good coffee than to drink bad coffee for free.' I'm trying to be friendly. She rolls her eyes.

She starts to make the coffee in a polystyrene mug. 'Could I have it in a cup please?' There are real cups on top of the coffee machine. She stops what she's doing, looks at me.

'You want it in a cup?'

'Yes, please.' I stay patient and friendly and smiling. She clearly considers me to be a mental retard.

'A cup,' she says. She still hasn't moved. I nod, still smiling. The smile apparently confirms my retard status.

She sighs, gets a cup down from the machine. It is dusty, so she wipes it out and puts the coffee in it. I sign the check (adding a fifteen per cent tip) and take my coffee to my table, stir some sugar into it with the plastic straw. It is a perfect coffee, everything about it is just right. I enjoy it, with a cigarette, despite the noise and the cold. I approach the stall once again. 'That was so good I'd like another one just the same please.'

Whether out of spite or for some other reason, the second coffee is not 'just the same.' It's terrible. There's nothing I can do about it, I've already done too much to her.

>>>>>>>>>>>>>>>>

That's the story of this hotel. They finally find my waiting faxes thirty-six hours after I arrive. Three times I've been promised that a power-point adapter will be delivered to my room, but none has yet arrived (there's another whole story with this one). A packet of cashews from the minibar costs eighteen Australian dollars. Room service is too expensive, I don't have enough clothes to eat in the hotel (it is literally too cold to sit down there for any length of time), and not enough American cash to go out (the banks are closed and the hotel doesn't know what overseas money is).

Outside is also bad, but in a different way. It's sleazy, dirty, unpleasant. People walk around exuding unhappiness. I buy a spinach quiche at a 'French' patisserie near the hotel (breakfast was hardly breakfast). Before I can say anything, it is folded into a huge sheet of paper, put into a large paper bag with four paper serviettes, and then the whole thing is put into a plastic bag for me to carry off. I spend minutes at a garbage bin unearthing the quiche from its wrappings. It is cold anyway. It's America.

Things get so bad that I am paralysed into inaction. I start to watch TV, truly a sign of degradation and depression. At random intervals of between five and fifteen minutes the television set spontaneously turns itself off. The minutes in between, the programs, are worse, a culture in complete decay, ghastly, terrible, shocking, obsessed with death and killing, the actuality channels bleating about how terrible it is (and profiting from it), the drama channels (owned by the same people) glorying in it.

There's a new form of censorship here, where they blur, soften really, any section of the image that is remotely sexual … then you flick channels to see someone hacked to death or shot, the image presented in perfect clarity.

It is a society that is slowly poisoning itself. It aggressively exports itself to the rest of the world and the rest of the world is willingly buying it. It is profoundly depressing.

Eventually, gratefully, it gets dark. Three of the lights in my room don't work. I go out to eat, after a day of a pastry and a cold spinach quiche. I find a cheap-looking sort of Italian restaurant, a little rundown but not too cold inside and you can smoke and get a drink. I decide to risk the Visa card.

I order a half bottle of Chianti and a *pasta e fagioli* (bean soup). They don't have the Chianti. I order a half bottle of something else. They come back without that as well. Finally they bring me the only half bottle of anything they have. Even though it's $12.95, in desperation I take it.

The soup comes. The bowl has been overfilled and the plate beneath it is swimming. The waitress smiles and says she's sorry. I continue my un-American activities by being nice.

I then taste the soup.

It is sensational. Not just good, but sensational. I order penne with broccoli. The penne itself is overcooked to buggery but apart from that the dish is very good. Then I order another bowl of bean soup. Again overfilled on a swimming plate. Again sensational.

Miami Diary

The whole eating experience puts me into a somewhat better frame of mind, and I find myself hoping Dreyfuss doesn't want to have dinner with me tomorrow night so that I can come back here and have more bean soup. It is something to look forward to in this godforsaken country.

In Search of a Dolphin's Grave

BILL BENNETT

Bill Bennett is regarded as one of Australia's most experienced and respected filmmakers. In a career spanning nearly thirty years, he's made fifteen feature films and more than forty documentaries. He's won numerous prizes internationally, had three major film retrospectives, and won Australian Film Institute Awards (Australia's Oscars) for Best Picture and Best Director. His filmmaking has taken him to many countries, including remote regions of Papua New Guinea, India, China and Africa.

I looked at my crumpled plastic bottle of water. It was a 1.5-litre bottle that I'd casually picked up that morning before setting off. I'd already drunk two-thirds. I'd gulped it down, unthinking, uncaring, on the long trip from Assab out to the edge of the Red Sea, bouncing through the scorched Eritrean desert past villages decimated by drought and famine, not realizing that as the day unraveled, every drop would become precious.

Outside the Land Rover it was in the mid-fifties (degrees Celsius, or about 130 degrees Fahrenheit). That's what my driver estimated at any rate. Even for him, that was hot. Heat that hot is not definable. It's not sweating hot. It's not dry-mouth hot. It's not put-the-air-con-to-max hot. It's blast-furnace hot. It's iron-smelter hot. It's melt-the-plastic-on-the-dashboard hot. Coming from Sydney, I thought hot was sitting on the beach at Bondi on Boxing Day, getting sunburnt and hoping for a sea breeze.

The Land Rover was bogged – bogged up to its chassis. It had broken through a thick mud crust and had sunk down into moist gloop, with the Red Sea only meters away, steam rising from the water as if from the spout of a boiling kettle. It was that hot. It was so hot I couldn't breathe through my mouth. It was like breathing air from a raging bushfire.

It scorched my throat and I had to breathe through my nose in short sharp gasps because getting a deep lungful of that incendiary air was hurtful. The heat burnt off the moisture on my eyeballs and I had to squint. My tongue was thickening and my lips were as cracked as the dried mud underfoot, or under-chassis.

The local young men who'd come along as guides, four in total, tried to push the long-wheelbase vehicle out but all that did was entrench it even further. We'd passed a village about ten kilometers back, but in this heat, walking ten kilometers would not be possible. No-one knew where we were, I'd foolishly not given my travel plans to anyone, and there was no such thing as a GPS rescue transmitter in our kit. We could simply perish out here in the firestorm heat in this isolated corner of Ethiopia and no-one would be the wiser for weeks, months or possibly even years.

The driver, Tommy, spoke English and he was flummoxed. He explained to me that the ground that we'd been driving along for the past hour or so – the flat bitumen-like foreshore – was in fact dried mud and when we stopped, the weight of the vehicle simply forced the tires through the thick crust, resting the chassis on top. Underneath was a thick muddy stew.

Normally when the vehicle gets bogged, he explained, he can either winch it out or find some foliage or branches to put under the tires to get some traction, but where we were, on this remote edge of the Red Sea, there were no trees or rocks to winch off, nothing to put under the tires except some odd stones, which immediately sank down into the gloop. The Land Rover was sitting belly flat on the cracked-chocolate mud and we were buggered.

I started to think of my wife and young family back in Sydney – wondering seriously if I would ever see them again. My only comfort was that the Hollywood producer who had sent me on this crazy quest to find a real-life mermaid had, on my request, taken out a life insurance policy. At least if I died in this parched cauldron, my family would get something.

It was a great story and would make a great film. The book was called *A Grave for a Dolphin,* a true story evidently written by an Italian cartographer sent to the Eritrean coast prior to World War II to chart the waters in preparation for an invasion by Mussolini's navy. Whilst there, he became deranged by heat exhaustion and loneliness, and woke up one morning to find a beautiful half-naked Maasai woman seeking shelter from slave traders. According to this man's diary, the woman turned out to be a dolphin, in love with another dolphin which would leap out of the warm waters of the Red Sea of an evening, to catch her eye.

I won't go into the details of the book, other than to say the woman-dolphin finally died, and the cartographer buried her in a rocky cairn on the edge of the Red Sea, near the border with Djibouti. There were enough clues in the book for me to attempt to find this cairn, and verify the story.

I had been contacted by this highly successful Hollywood producer to write and direct the film. I read the book and realized that to write a screenplay with any degree of reality and to avoid cliché, I really needed to go to Eritrea to steep myself in the culture, the language, the nuances of the place and the people, and to try and find this grave. This would then give me the background texture to write a fully dimensional screenplay.

The producer admired greatly my professionalism, understanding that it would make the script much richer and hence easier for him to finance with a studio, and yet highly successful though he was, wealthy beyond my immediate understanding, every day doing deals in six- and seven-digit figures, he would not spring for my travel costs, flying coach-class even. The cost of my trip would have been equivalent to a big dinner for some studio heads at Spago. But nope, it was 'on your dime,' as he put it. Welcome to Hollywood.

At the time I had a young family and not many dimes. I felt though that this was a great opportunity to write something of real merit and so my wife agreed to my going, on the condition that the producer take out life insurance in case anything went wrong. We'd just bought a new house, populated with newish babies, and Eritrea was a minor war zone, even though the area where I was going was out of the conflict. The producer agreed to the insurance – I did my medicals, signed my forms – and so off I went, first to Addis Ababa, then to Assab, near the coast.

There was only one real hotel in Assab and that was more like a firebombed concrete bunker. My room had a bed of sorts, a shower of sorts, cement floors with no coverings, and no curtains on the windows. Not that anyone would want to look in.

The shower had only one tap – cold – and I soon realized that was because there was no need for hot water. The cold water came out near boiling – presumably because the water ran through pipes in the ground, and the ground was almost too hot to walk on. The water was so hot I had to let it run into a plastic bucket, kindly supplied by the hotel, and then let it cool before I could splash it over myself.

Outside of the town were fenced-in compounds containing dozens of old army tanks and missile-launching vehicles, all ravaged by the desert and past wars. Even though Assab was south of the Eritrean capital, Asmara, where most of the fighting was happening, there were soldiers everywhere.

The town was also full of aid workers, a veritable army of professional NGO-ers looking after famine relief for the surrounding districts. The drought had been endless, and the country was denuded of all living vegetation, other than a few stunted trees and some brave cacti. The Eritreans themselves were stick thin, and yet everywhere people ran. They ran down the dusty streets, they ran in the mornings and in the evenings, they ran barefoot over ground that was so hot I needed thick-soled, asbestos-lined Timberlands. This, I realized, is why

Ethiopia has such extraordinary long-distance athletes, because instead of lazing around in their shanties watching ESPN on television or kicking back by the oasis reading a book, they're out running.

I arranged to have some local guides take me further south towards the border with Djibouti, towards the place where I believed the grave to be. Despite the cost, the hardship of being there, the danger and the overbearing heat, I was driven by the deliciousness of this story. Could it be true that this forgotten corner of the world had seas harboring dolphins that can transmogrify into women? True mermaids?

I was determined to find out.

We set off the next morning. I'd grabbed a bottle of water just before leaving, from a place purporting to be Assab's version of a 7-Eleven. We headed out of town, past the graveyard of tanks, past the roadblocks manned by bored soldiers with old-fashioned machine guns that probably didn't work, past the sinewy young barefoot men running out into the fiery desert just because they loved running.

When we left that morning, the temperature was forty-nine degrees Celsius. That's 120 degrees Fahrenheit. A couple of my guides had jumpers on, it was so chilly. They didn't start to warm up until it got beyond fifty-four degrees Celsius.

The wind was cutting. It gave the heat sharp edges that sliced into my lips, scoured my eyes. Even so, we were heading into exotic territory – towards the Red Sea, the Arabian Gulf. I'd read before leaving Sydney that scientists believed the Red Sea had, through quirks of ancient geophysical activity, become something of a closed ecosystem containing species that existed nowhere else on earth. Could it be that this hermetically sealed aquarium housed real mermaids?

The Land Rover was a relic, even though it was costing me an eye-watering amount to hire for the day. It was long wheelbased, without any such genteel accessories as air-con or radio, but it trundled easily along the tracks and paths that led us to the coast of the Red Sea, past villages of dour thatched huts with beautiful women wearing brightly colorful cloth that billowed in the hot wind.

There were no crops, no wells, no workable agriculture or stock. There was just sun-blasted desert and rocky hills with spiky weed and these statuesque resolute people who inhabited this uninhabitable land.

We got to the coast several hours later. The ground gave way to a tarmac-like flat, which took us right out to the edge of the sea. I was hoping that I could have a swim because the temperature had climbed to the mid-fifties and I had already drunk half my water.

I'd been expecting dazzling white sands leading to deep blue sparkling waters, some coral maybe, reefs offshore with exotic birdlife, dolphins frolicking, turtles breaking surface and gulping air, schools of swarming fish rippling across the Gulf. In other words, I had this wildly romantic notion of what the Red Sea would be like.

What greeted me at the edge of the sea was something quite different – a baked mudflat that was quickly consumed by a thick rolling wall of mist, or rather steam, rising in whorls from the water. I could barely see fifty meters out past the shoreline. And the dirty turgid sea, when I tried to swim in it, was so hot it was like a spa on steroids. This was not a refreshing dunk in sweet crystalline waters. This was a breathless fetid dip in murky swirling heat-fog.

I quickly got back into the vehicle and we headed further south, now following the coastline, watching out for any rock formations that could possibly be the cairn where the woman-dolphin had been buried. We stopped several times and I jumped out, ran over, checked out a hillock or pile of rocks, but they all seemed to be just that, a hillock or pile of rocks. Not something this love-struck delirious Italian mapmaker had constructed to be the mausoleum for his magical creature.

As we approached what must have been the border with Djibouti – because out here, there were no customs and immigration gates, no cheery signpost saying 'You are now leaving Ethiopia, have a nice day' – there was only a sense that you'd driven far enough and the bordering country just had to be not far off – it was then that I spotted a jutting finger of land prodding out into the Gulf. I remembered a similar description in the book, the place where the mapmaker had camped.

I told Tommy to drive out, and as we approached, I saw a massive pile of rocks. In the book, the cartographer had described how he'd buried the woman, carrying rocks from surrounding hills. We stopped. I got out and walked over.

What was I hoping to find? Bones? Fish bones? The sun-bleached skeletal remains of a woman's head and a fish's tail? A headstone with an inscription: 'Rest in Peace Oh Dolphin Girl.'

All I found was a big pile of rocks where there should never have been a pile of rocks. It made no sense for that pile of rocks to be there. It looked man-made. If I really squinted, it looked slightly Italian. Possibly even from the Milanese School of Rock Design. Hah. Who knew? It could have been the grave, but then again it could have been put there by fishermen as a beacon. Or it could have been freakishly washed up by unseasonal weather. I would never know.

I took pictures so the Hollywood producer would know that I got there, then I walked back to the Land Rover and saw that we were bogged.

It took us four hours to dig the Land Rover out with our hands. And I really did think that I was going to die. As I scooped out gloop with my fingers, on my knees at the back wheels with that furnace heat enveloping my entire being with its suffocating stupor, I began to think of my wife, my young children, our new house, and the insurance that would keep them going after they found my body, shrivelled to a dried prune somewhere out in the deserts of southern Eritrea.

There would probably be a funeral in the church where all the film people in Sydney have funerals, and there would be a few articles, maybe in the local trades. The local television station might run a couple of my films as a memorial, most probably at 1:30am. Would my death make *Variety*? I hoped so. These things I considered as I scooped gloop.

We finally got the vehicle moving, the dark coming on, and I was so weak with heat exhaustion and lack of hydration that I'd started to hallucinate. I'd finished my water hours earlier, and so we made our way further south to a fishing village close to the border, hoping they'd have some.

The village was a cluster of small huts and houses, all painted the most vivid pastel colors, huddled around a small raised hill overlooking the gulf. The colors were a marker for distant fishing boats, to find their way home. They offered me some water pulled from a near empty well. It wasn't water so much as gruel. It was like the slop that I'd hauled out from under the Land Rover. But it was liquid, of sorts, and I gulped down as much as my stomach would allow.

A few days later, on returning to Addis Ababa, I would be bedridden in my room in the Hilton – unable to move for a couple of weeks.

But at the village, after slaking my thirst with the dregs of the well, the driver Tommy took me down to the water's edge, where a group of fishermen were sitting around a smoky fire in the growing gloom, patching their nets.

Through a translator I asked the old men if they'd heard through story or myth about an Italian man who'd come to their area a couple of generations earlier, and met a woman who he believed to be a dolphin.

The men laughed and laughed. We see them all the time, they said. The women fish. They foul our nets. We always have to repair our nets, they are such a nuisance.

I sat there in the dim light stunned. Were they serious? Or were they having a gigantic lend of me? They didn't seem to be mischievous or tricksters – they had no reason to lie, there was no financial gain for them.

'When did this last happen?' I asked them.

The head man, an old wizened weather-beaten fellow, thought back, talked to his mates, and said a couple of months ago. He said it was like a fish, but it had the breasts and the genitals of a woman.

Was this a dugong, I wondered – often mistaken for a creature that's half woman and half fish? Surely there had to be a logical and scientific explanation. The old man told me that they'd caught this creature and skinned it. It was hanging up in one of their houses on the edge of the village.

'Can I see it?' I immediately asked. I could then tell if they'd skinned a Maasai tribeswoman or a dugong. It was grizzly, yes, but at least after coming all this way, I would know. But Tommy was getting antsy. It was near on dark now, and there was a curfew back at town. We had to go or else risk getting shot or imprisoned. I pleaded, implored, offered money, but Tommy was resolute. We had to get going straight away. So I never did get to see the dried hanging skin of a mermaid – or perhaps a dugong.

I got back to Assab before the curfew and raced to the shower to try to cool down, given that the air-con in the room was an illusory joke. However, when I stood under the tap, I screamed. I thought perhaps I'd turned on the hot tap by mistake but there was no hot tap. The cold water could boil eggs.

Next morning I flew back to Addis Ababa, unsure as to what I'd actually achieved. Was the rocky pile really the grave? I liked to think so, but then again, I'd once liked to think that the Red Sea was blue too. And were the fishermen telling the truth about the female sea creatures who fouled their nets? Certainly this was a part of the world where you could believe anything – even the most fantastical – and if it was true that the Gulf had become a closed ecosystem, might it not be true that real mermaids swam its murky depths?

The water that I'd chewed at the village was full of bugs and parasites, and I got very sick – so sick I couldn't fly out of Ethiopia. But on a local doctor's advice I began eating homegrown yogurt and that either killed the bugs or confused them, because soon I was able to return to Australia.

When I got back, I called Hollywood and I told the producer of my adventures. He was fascinated, of course, as all Hollywood producers are when they talk to writers, and even more intrigued when I told him of how I'd got stuck in the desert and nearly died. I said I was thankful for the life insurance policy because that had given me some solace in those direst of moments.

The producer laughed. It was the kind of laugh you'd hear from a robotic sideshow clown just before you put a ball in its mouth. 'You did take out the life insurance, didn't you?' I asked him. 'Oh yes,' he replied, still chortling. 'Except too bad you made it back because I made myself the beneficiary. I coulda financed my next picture.' I concluded the call with him still laughing.

The film never got made. The producer lost the rights; I heard they went to Bertolucci's producer and he never made it either. But hey, it was a great trip.

Egyptian Magic

ANTHONY SATTIN

Anthony Sattin is the author of several highly acclaimed books on history and travel, and a leading travel journalist, identified by *Condé Nast Traveller* as one of ten key influences on travel writing today. His books include *The Pharaoh's Shadow*, *Shooting the Breeze*, *Lifting the Veil*, *The Gates of Africa* and *A Winter on the Nile*. He discovered and edited Florence Nightingale's previously unpublished letters from Egypt and co-edited the anthology *A House Somewhere: Tales of Life Abroad*. He has been a long time regular contributor to the *Sunday Times* travel and books pages and to *Condé Nast Traveller*. His work has appeared in a number of other international publications, including the *Daily Telegraph*, the *Independent* and the *Guardian*. He sits on the editorial advisory board of *Geographical* magazine and has contributed to several guidebook series, including Lonely Planet's *Egypt* and *Algeria*. He has also written and presented on television and radio, including several high-profile documentaries for BBC Radio 3 and 4.

The café was just back from the waterfront. The evening was hot and humid, the lights foggy with Mediterranean brine. There was a constant stream of people along the pavement and the café was busy, so it wasn't long before someone asked if they could join me at my table. I moved the glass hub of my water pipe aside and gestured to the seat beside me. *Atfaddal.* Help yourself. He did and, since he was Egyptian, it wasn't long before he began a conversation.

'From where? England? What brings you to my city?'

The opening was familiar. I had heard it a dozen times that day and wondered whether everyone in the city had had a briefing about how to address a foreigner.

When the conversation had run its course – my job, my family, the price of cigarettes – I asked the one question I needed answered.

The man, who was a teacher, looked puzzled. As he said nothing in reply, I had a moment to watch his face. I could see he was turning over the options, before choosing the most obvious.

Had he heard me correctly?

'Yes,' I assured him. 'I am looking for a magician.'

'Are you in trouble?'

'Not yet,' but I would be if I didn't find one – and very soon – for I had just one day left in the city.

I had been to Alexandria on other occasions, for many different reasons. It was a place I had gone to have fun, to do research and to make irrevocable decisions about my future. Once, I was even sent there by my doctor, in summer, to recover from a bout of typhoid. 'The sea air will do you good,' he had assured me, and he was right. It did. And now I was there to fulfill a commission from a television production company that wanted me to look for magicians in Egypt. I'll come to the why of it in a minute.

'So why,' asked my café companion, 'do you want a magician?' I explained about the television program and that I had heard that there was one particularly skilled practitioner in Alexandria. I had come to the city to find him, but after several days of looking, I had drawn a blank.

The man told me not to worry. He didn't know of one himself, but he thought he knew someone who did. He would make enquiries and suggested we meet again the following evening, when he hoped to have a lead. In most countries this would seem like a lost cause, but life in Egypt is often strange and wonderful, and the unlikely is never impossible. I'll give you an example. A while back, I was in a Cairo taxi, stuck in the usual mire of traffic, when the driver burst into tears. You and I can think of several reasons why a Cairene taxi driver might want to cry: the traffic, low earnings and high pollution levels being just three. But when I asked what was wrong, he told me that he wasn't a driver. He was an accountant. He had borrowed the car from a friend because he needed to make money in a hurry. His wife had been badly hurt; a gas canister had exploded while she was cooking in their kitchen. He needed money to pay for the operation that would save her. Was there anything I could do to help? I gave, of course. There was a report in the news the next day about a woman hurt by an exploding canister. But that didn't prove that the woman in the story was the wife of the taxi driver.

>>>>>>>>>>>>>>>

The following evening, back at the waterfront café, my fellow tea-drinker was there with a smile on his face. 'I have an address. I know where to go.' We would have to wait until a little later, he assured me, though as the hours went by I realized that this was as much for him to smoke his water pipe and tell his stories as it was for the magician to arrive at his home.

Eventually we took a tram, a rattling remnant of the colonial age, and headed out east through four or five stops of unremitting crowds and concrete. We then turned inland on foot for a while until we stopped in front of a nineteenth-century building. This neighborhood was rundown, and so was the house, so much so that it wasn't until we got inside that I realized it was derelict.

We walked up the unlit, broken, littered staircase to the third and uppermost floor. There was only one door off the landing. We knocked and waited, knocked again and entered. The door opened onto a void: the floor had fallen in and been replaced by some planks leading away from the door. Lit by light from the street, I could see that on the other side of the room there was another door. We crossed very carefully and entered the magician's room.

Whatever might be said about this man of tricks, he was certainly neat. Equally certain was the fact that he was asleep when we walked in. He had electricity and when he switched on his bedside light, I took in the room. It contained a large brass bed, a chest of drawers and a massive wardrobe. The remaining floor space was taken up by myself and my guide.

The magician was a man in his fifties, tall and wiry, his hair still black. His name was Bafa and he was clearly down on his luck, living alone in this ruin, occasionally being paid to brighten up a children's party, eking out a very meagre living. When I explained why I had come, that I was looking for the roots of Egyptian magic for a television show, he had a feeling he had just won the lottery. He sat up, rolled an old newspaper into a cone, took the recycled plastic water bottle off his chest of drawers and poured its contents into the paper, which he then handed to me. When I opened it, the paper was dry, the water nowhere to be found.

'I can do more. I can do better,' he assured me, 'but I need a little time to prepare.'

Time was one thing I couldn't give him; in the morning, I had to leave for the south and before leaving, I had many questions to ask. Who was he? How had he come by his skills? How long had he been practising? Where did he perform? But he had no use for words and he ignored my questions. Instead, he lit a cigarette, took a deep draw on it and then swallowed the butt. He opened his gaseous mouth to show that it was empty, then opened it again and the butt reappeared.

I wished he could do the same with time. 'But I will come back and then you can show me your skills.'

I headed south.

>>>>>>>>>>>>>>

The program's producers had raised a significant amount of money by promising to take some of the world's most famous magicians in search of the origins of Western magic. Their production team had spent time trying to make contact with Egyptian magicians, or at least to do some background research, and had got nowhere. Knowing that I had undertaken my own hunt for magicians for my book *The Pharaoh's Shadow,* they had asked if I could help.

The Pharaoh's Shadow was an account of my search for the surviving culture of ancient Egypt. It was an attempt to answer a single question. We know that so much of the fabric of ancient Egypt has survived in the form of its temples and tombs. But what of the life that had been lived around them? Magic was an everyday part of ancient life. Each part of the day, each stage of life and death was wrapped in, and shored up by, magic. Spells were used to ensure the pharaoh would reach the afterlife. Religion was also heavily dependent on tricks, magic turns that ensured the pharaoh heard the voice of the gods when he entered the holy sanctuaries alone. When Christians finally stormed the great pagan temple of Serapis in Alexandria in the fourth century, the mob hesitated in front of the massive figure of the god: they had never been so close to divinity before and they knew of the warning that if a mere mortal should approach the statue, the city would be struck by an earthquake, a serious matter in that region. The zealous bishop, later described as 'a bald, bad man, whose hands were alternately polluted with gold and with blood,' finally broke the spell when he had the god beheaded and its body toppled. The levers that had given the god 'life' were exposed, the trick was up, the god was dead. To prove it, the zealots dragged the body through the streets, burning parts in different quarters of the city.

Christianity frowned on magic, even though one of its central moments, the communion when bread and wine were turned into flesh and blood, was clearly part of this ancient tradition of religious magic. Islam seemed to have been more tolerant and for much of the 1400 years since the Arab invasion, magic remained a key part of everyday life along the Nile. From a belief in a spirit double – an avatar – that lived alongside our earthly bodies, to a certainty that some special people could summon significant powers, magic was still common in Egypt. If a woman had difficulty conceiving, she would go first to the doctor, then to the imam of her mosque. If that didn't work, she would then supplicate other powers. She might take herself to one of the ancient temples or shrines, and roll on the floor, wash herself in fetid water from a sacred lake or merely beg the ancient gods for help. Or she might go to a healer, who would prescribe a ritual involving vaginal suppositories and water from the Nile.

I knew how productions worked and knew that none of these rituals could, or should, make it onto television. I toyed with the idea of finding a snake charmer, perhaps one of the Rifai Sufi sect who were said to have been initiated into a mystery that allowed them to handle snakes without fear. I looked for a levitation expert and was introduced to a Cairene theatrical agent who received me, at 10pm, in his bedroom. His wife sat beside him in her nightgown as naturally as though she were fully dressed and we were sitting in an office (the bedroom was his office). 'This sort of act,' and he stretched his hand flat on the bedcover and slowly lifted it towards the ceiling, 'is increasingly difficult to stage. People don't come to the shows like they used to. Who can compete with TV and computer games?' He had a point: when I finally saw the act, at a village fair, it was unconvincing.

Then I heard of a Sufi who lived in a tomb in the City of the Dead, and could put himself into a trance and drive a spike through his cheek without either pain or blood.

The man was understandably loath to perform for me; his act was one of devotion, not of entertainment. A century earlier, on holy days, Cairo's streets were full of extraordinary spectacles, one of which involved a line of Sufi devotees placing daggers in their mouths while their sheikh walked along the hilts, without harming them. Other Sufis lay on the ground, in a trance, while their sheikh rode over them on his horse, again without causing any apparent harm. But the government had become suspicious of this sort of esoterica and had banned public displays of this sort. Although I did manage to persuade him to show me his feat – performed in his tomb-home, in a trance, with the man wearing a green robe – and still don't know how it was achieved, it was clear that this too would never make it onto the screen. And then I went back to Alexandria.

>>>>>>>>>>>>>>>>

Through the man who had introduced us, I sent a message to Bafa, asking him to prepare his feats and offering to pay him well for the performance. A message came back: he would be waiting for me on the corniche, near the fishermen's mosque. I took the train to the north coast full of expectation.

Bafa had suggested meeting at sundown, that moment at the end of a hot day, celebrated in the same way around the Mediterranean, when people come out of their houses to take the air and to take time to greet each other. Swallows wheeled overhead, the broad sweep of the harbor was clogged with traffic, a line of fishing boats were tied up on the greasy water. The landside pavement was crowded with families, the children and mothers running and shouting. Among them was a single, motionless, magnificent point. It was Bafa.

He stood in front of a small table at the back of the broad walkway. On his head he wore a turban. It was of gold fabric, which matched the gilding of his waistcoat and the seam of his clean, baggy trousers. He looked magnificent. In his hand he held a large drum. As he beat it, drumming up business, a circle began to form around him, small at first, but soon filling out as he announced the imminence of his show. By the time he stopped banging, there were perhaps fifty or sixty people in front of him, ready for whatever was to come.

The tricks were the stock-in-trade of the circus magician, sleights of hand and extravagant gestures that had us all cheering and clapping. As they followed one after the other, the crowd was transformed. For those brief moments, adults forgot about their troubles, about the cars crawling past, the honking horns, and remembered their childhood. Children were reminded of the power of suggestion. But the biggest transformation, bigger even than the rabbit that was turned into a pigeon, was of the magician himself. For as long as his performance lasted, Bafa was wreathed in a majestic light. He stood taller. He smiled. The cares of his failing life were forgotten. There on the Alexandria waterfront, the greatest trick of all was the reinvention of the trickster.

Then the loudspeakers on the front of the fishermen's mosque crackled into life and, as the faithful were called to prayer, the crowd began to slip away. Bafa knew what this meant, that his moment had passed, and made one last extravagant gesture, taking a low bow while there were still people to applaud. He smiled at me. And I smiled back, my job done.

The Magic Garden of Nek Chand

PAUL COX

Born in Holland, Paul Cox migrated to Australia in the mid-1960s as a trained photographer and went on to become one of the country's most prolific, individualistic and internationally acclaimed filmmakers. Over a 35-year filmmaking career, the signature traits of Cox's work are a deep humanism, a poignant and realistic focus on relationships, eclecticism, and a profound affinity with the arts. An international film festival favorite whose retrospectives include New York's prestigious Lincoln Center for the Performing Arts, Cox is one of the true independent filmmakers in contemporary cinema.

My friend Ulli Beier returned one day from a trip to India and showed me photographs he'd taken in a garden in Chandigarh. This was not an ordinary garden. It was called the 'Rock Garden' and Ulli's slides showed a glimpse into a world of magic and beauty that one encounters in strange dreams and strange hallucinations. Endless rows of queens and kings, horsemen, wild animals and other creatures known and unknown standing on hills, in ponds, hiding in exotic temples, alleyways and archways.

The person responsible for creating this Rock Garden was an amazing artist called Nek Chand. I remember having a wild dream that night and something or someone told me, 'Go there immediately, make a film, make a record, and preserve this miracle.' The message had an urgency that surprised me.

Ulli told me that Nek Chand's creation had been under siege several times. Nek Chand had claimed government land and a politician had tried to call in the bulldozers to reclaim the land. Fortunately this had been fought by local supporters and friends, but the garden remained under threat. I felt urgently compelled to record it for posterity!

But filmmaking is not like any of the other arts. It requires money, people, rights, scripts. And where do you find the money and the people to invest in something as mysterious and exotic as a so-called 'rock garden?' There wasn't much time and we both had other commitments.

We decided to just do it! I was still teaching at the time and asked a fellow teacher, Bryan Gracey, to carry the lights. I had an old camera and managed to find enough rolls of Kodak film for our task ahead.

We bought three cheap tickets to New Delhi and within a fortnight we were on our way. In Delhi there were no trains to take us to Chandigarh. There were some political problems in the Punjab. We found a taxi driver who promised he would get us there 'in no time.'

The approximately 150-kilometer trip took us two days! Apart from the car losing several parts on the bumpy roads, there were other problems I won't go into. We stayed overnight at a very cheap inn and as we were munching away at our fried rice, a rat appeared and casually found a place in the window behind Ulli's back.

Ulli was a wonderful storyteller and barely flinched when I told him that a rat was staring at his left ear and was trying to put his front legs on his shoulder. Then three other large rats appeared and started to fight on the floor of the small restaurant. They were really large and even the local people were standing on tables and chairs to avoid getting involved!

The next day we found our rock garden. It had been a bit of an ordeal to get there, but the first sight of the garden and meeting its creator made us forget everything. When we arrived, there was an old sadhu sitting on a hill. He was wearing the same colors as the statues that surrounded him. Then he sang an old devotional song from the very heart of India and we became too mesmerized to move. The singing of that old man has always traveled with me.

Nek Chand, a humble man, had been working as a road inspector near Chandigarh when he had a vivid dream of a vast kingdom on the very site of which he was in charge. For the next eight years he labored to convert this wasteland into the magic kingdom of his dream. Working day and night after normal working hours, he gathered and transported on his bicycle stones, rocks and urban waste. He retrieved old cycles and unusable parts from cycle shops. He burned old bicycle tyres to give him light at night. He collected used factory drums and broken crockery from restaurants and cafés. He collected buckets full of broken bangles thrown away after festivals. Out of all this garbage, broken articles of daily use, pebbles and stones, he built his kingdom.

Beginning with the king's throne, the original dream expanded. The garden grew and grew, quietly, never requiring the purchase of materials, subsidy, or advice. Art for art's sake, for no reward, no recognition during the long years in solitude.

The garden remained a secret until it was discovered eight years after its conception by government employees spraying against malaria on the outskirts of the city. The discovery so moved officials that they began to help Nek Chand. Some politicians complained about a government employee using public land, but this narrow-mindedness was soon ignored. The Rock Garden was formally inaugurated in 1976 and since then people from all over the world have visited this strange, almost living work of art, a wonderland of rare artistic merit created entirely from waste material. The director of the Musée d'Art Moderne in Paris wrote in Nek Chand's visitor book, 'God has a competitor – his name is Nek Chand.'

No visitor entering this magic garden remains unmoved. Children gaze enthralled; adults are mesmerized. This is the work of a single obsessive human being, an artist of great instinctive integrity. I've watched people visiting Disneyland, and I've sat for days high on the wall of Nek Chand's kingdom, watching its visitors. No doubt Disneyland is enchanting, but the people leave it spiritually empty-handed. Here in Nek Chand's garden they are enriched to such a degree that they leave quietly, holding hands, smiling. They've shared something of magic and beauty that will nourish their dreams for many years to come.

Paul Cox

Ulli Beier died recently. He was also a man of magic. What a great privilege it was to have known him and to have traveled with him. From him I learned to look at the world openly and humbly without making a face. He taught and inspired thousands of students around the world, from Nigeria to New Guinea, Germany to Australia. Our little film *The Kingdom of Nek Chand* is now dedicated to his memory and to all those who inspire, treasure and honor the creative force within all of us.

The Wonders of Whitby

NEIL LABUTE

Neil LaBute is a writer and director for film, theater and television. His projects include *In the Company of Men*, *Bash*, *The Shape of Things*, *Your Friends & Neighbors*, *The Distance from Here*, *Filthy Talk for Troubled Times*, *Nurse Betty*, *Fat Pig*, *The Break of Noon*, *Possession*, *Wrecks*, *Autobahn*, *This is How it Goes*, *The Wicker Man*, *The Mercy Seat*, *In a Dark Dark House*, *Lakeview Terrace*, *Death at a Funeral*, *In a Forest, Dark and Deep*, and *Some Girl(s)*. He is also the author of the short story collection *Seconds of Pleasure*.

If you happen to find yourself on the northern coast of England making a motion picture (as I did a few years ago), then be sure to put the town of Whitby at the top of your list of 'places I need to visit on the northern coast of England while I make a motion picture.' Or you might want to visit one day for no apparent reason, which I would happily suggest to virtually anyone who enjoys England, the outdoors or any place remotely beautiful.

I was lucky enough to spend a few days in Yorkshire while working on an adaptation of AS Byatt's *Possession*. A good portion of the novel is set in this lovely northern community and we were lucky enough to film various scenes on or near the actual locations suggested in her book.

Whitby is a rugged and handsome community, perched on the mouth of the River Esk as it reaches the North Sea. It is a place of extreme juxtapositions and it is an amazing place to 'people watch' as the locals, tourists and goths mix freely in the streets. The sheer number and variety of 'types' you see walking down the narrow avenues of Whitby is reward enough for stopping there, but there is much more to enjoy for the day visitor or someone who plans to spend a few days in the region.

One of the best places to start is high above the town – 199 steps, to be exact, up a beautifully weathered stone staircase – at the ruins of Whitby Abbey, which was the inspiration for parts of the classic novel *Dracula*. In fact, Bram Stoker stayed in Whitby while writing his most famous work and his attention to local detail is apparent in the pages of his story. The Abbey is now visited by flocks of tourists but it is the huge influx of 'goths' (a wide net that includes vampire enthusiasts, people who are drawn to the clothes and trappings of a 'gothic' lifestyle and many others) who have turned this area into a local mecca for the macabre. Whitby itself has embraced the black-garbed visitors and now has twice-yearly festivals, 'Goth

Weekends,' that are major tourist attractions and rank high on the calendars of gothic-themed events around the world.

Just below the ruins of the Abbey itself is one of my favorite sites in all of Whitby. There is a little parish church just near the top of the stairs on the east cliff of the town where a stunning graveyard sits. The headstones number among the most singular and haunting I have ever seen (and I do love looking at headstones). The faces of these stone monuments have all been nearly worn away by the rough sea air and the salt has created a jumble of lost words and memories. They really do have to be seen to be believed; I found them a moving and unforgettable tribute to people long since passed away.

Whitby is certainly known for many other treasures as well as its rich Victorian heritage in literature – many fossils have been found in the nearby cliffs, and jet (a kind of hard black mineraloid created by decaying wood) has been a standard form of minor gemstone since the reign of Queen Victoria. Even the Roman invaders mined the rich-looking material from the local area, but jet was made most famous by the Queen herself and it began to be used fashionably as an accessory in mourning dress. It is something that can be easily carved and shaped with detail so its use in jewelry grew greatly during the nineteenth century. Some beautiful examples are still in evidence in various shops in the old town of Whitby.

Wonderful ammonite fossils – or 'snake stones' – have also been unearthed in the steep valley and seaside cliffs surrounding the town. These are sold as religious souvenirs in various shops and gift stalls throughout Whitby, adding to the rich atmosphere and heritage of this delightful town. Nothing is more precious, though, than a simple walk down the alleys and twisting streets of Whitby itself. Each of the buildings in town seems to house a vast history, all the way down to the edge of the water where the twin piers lead you out into the great North Sea. The whole town feels like an adventure that one wants to take when they're young but will remember for a lifetime no matter when in life they do it.

A stop at the Magpie Café for amazing fish and chips is well worth your time, but you'll be getting your cod or halibut with the skin on one side, which is not my favorite way for it to be served. I'm a child of the 'fish sticks and Tater Tots' generation and I like my fish prepared like the good folks at Long John Silver's do it, with no portion of the actual fish in sight. The only time I've ever had fish and chips without the skin on in England was in the nearby northern town of Scarborough and frankly, it's worth the drive. Delicious chips ('French fries' to most Americans) are easy to come by, but a piece of batter-dipped fish without that dark skin on it is worth the travel (and there's also a lovely theater-in-the-round, the Stephen Joseph, in Scarborough that used to be run by the great English director and playwright Alan Ayckbourn).

Outside of town is a wonderful little train station and further up into the valley is the rugged countryside that leads back to the Yorkshire moors, which is where Ms Byatt imagined a fanciful meeting of her Victorian poets and present-day literary sleuths (at a beautiful small waterfall called Thomason Foss). Whitby is a terrific place to spend an afternoon or a weekend, and the thrills and delights are not just fictional ones, I promise you. Whitby is full of life and food and people whom you will remember long after you are safely back home and the coast of England is but a happy, distant memory.

I love London, but I adore Whitby. It is now what I dream of when I dream of England.

A Day in Istanbul

RICK STEVES

Rick Steves has spent a hundred days every year since 1973 exploring Europe. Rick produces a public television series, *Rick Steves' Europe,* a public radio show, *Travel with Rick Steves,* and a podcast, *Rick Steves' Audio Europe;* writes a bestselling series of guidebooks and a nationally syndicated newspaper column; organizes guided tours that take thousands of travelers to Europe annually; and offers an information-packed website, www.ricksteves.com. With the help of his hardworking staff of seventy at Europe Through the Back Door – in Edmonds, Washington, just north of Seattle – Rick's mission is to make European travel fun, affordable, and culturally broadening for Americans.

Standing in a commotion of commuters in a churning ferry terminal, I looked into the camera and said, 'Istanbul is one of the world's great cities, period. For thousands of years, this point, where East meets West, has been the crossroads of civilizations. Few places on earth have seen more history than this sprawling metropolis on the Bosphorus.'

But I wasn't happy with the shot. The site just wasn't right. Mentally scanning all possible angles, it hit me – we needed what filmmakers call a 'high-wide', a wide-angle, almost aerial shot. I wanted to show the freighter-filled Bosphorus and its Golden Horn inlet, the teeming Galata Bridge, lumbering commuter ferries churning up the port, and a huge mosque in the foreground. It was a lot to ask for.

We went to the spot I envisioned (above what the locals call the New Mosque, near the famous Spice Market) and surveyed the zone. A restaurant had a shaded roof terrace; we went there, and the view was fabulous, except there was no direct sunshine to light my face. With the bright vista in the background, that wouldn't work.

Next door, a toy company had offices with a small rooftop terrace in the sun. It was perfect. We explained our need, and they welcomed our crew onto their roof, brought us tea, and – grabbing a calm moment between gusts of wind – I delivered my lines.

Istanbul is rich in images and stories to tell. For this six-day shoot, we had enough material for two shows, but I decided I'd rather do a 'dense' Istanbul in half an hour, so some scenes had to be cut.

A Day in Istanbul

Simon Griffith, my producer-director, and I had to drop a sequence about merchants in the Grand Bazaar pitching their wares with goofy, sentimental and clever sales lines. Wandering through the market, I had an almost masochistic yearning to be hit with their desperate come-ons: 'Can I sell you something you don't need?' 'Love is blind but never mind.' 'Don't I know you?' 'Special price today ... just for you, my friend.'

I really wanted to capture that flirtatious montage on video. But with a big camera, the merchants clammed up. While some were simply shy, others seemed to have been burned recently by TV reporters doing negative stories. One guy said, 'You just want to make us look bad.' I said, 'No, I want to make you look good. Are you bad?' He said, 'We are bad, yes. But we don't want to look bad.'

Thankfully, my favorite market artisan did his time-honored craft candidly ... despite our camera. In the far end of the bazaar, the goldsmith was hard at work – melting scraps and sweepings into a little brick of solid gold. In three minutes, the gold went from loose shavings to molten metal poured into a mold, cooled in a bucket of water, polished with newspaper, and into my hands. Being the first to hold that brand-new, four-pound brick of gold in that funky, ramshackle, hot hole-in-the-wall was fun ... and great TV.

During the shoot, I tuned into the people around us. At first, there were cruise-ship passengers filling the Hippodrome square and the main street in the Grand Bazaar. When a perfect storm of cruise ships pulls into port, the tourist zones of the city are inundated with groups obediently following the numbered ping-pong paddles of their local guides. But then, by simply stepping into the thriving market streets beyond the tourist zone, the tourists were gone, replaced by a festival of telegenic local faces.

I'd always wanted to film Istanbul's fishing boat captains cooking up their catch right on their bobbing decks. They serve it in hunks of bread wrapped in newspaper. (This Istanbul fast food is a sentimental memory from my teenage visit here.) So I took the crew down to the waterfront. With the boats rocking wildly, we bought our sandwiches.

As I sat down to eat mine, a bird strafed me. It was as if yellow mustard (the expensive kind with grains in it) had just squirted out of the sky. A streak landed on my sleeve and another on the thigh of my pants. I heard a third squirt land in the vicinity of my sandwich. When I surveyed my fried mackerel, it was still the same color – rustic yellow – camouflaging whatever may have landed there.

Our local guide said, 'That's why we don't like pigeons.' Simon tried to comfort me, saying, 'It's probably mostly mackerel, anyway.' I still couldn't finish my fishy snack.

The slick new city tram – notoriously crowded throughout the day – was not jammed after rush hour. So we hopped on and filmed it as we returned to our hotel. We met a beautiful woman in a striking black scarf covered with bangles. I asked her husband where they were from, thinking Oman or Sudan or Timbuktu or someplace really exotic. He said, 'Istanbul.' I said, '*Çok güzel*' (very beautiful) while thinking, 'Fundamentalism is a growing presence even in modern Istanbul.'

Inspired to learn more about Muslim headwear, we dropped into a nearby scarf shop. All over Istanbul, I spied Muslim Britney Spears wannabes, covered up under scarves. There's some hypocrisy going on here: you know, they wear high heels and thongs ... but their heads are covered. In the fine silk shop, a young woman demonstrated scarf-wrapping techniques. One way looks flirtatious; another is simply demure and conservative. I pressed the saleswoman to show me the fundamentalist Muslim style. She tied it under her chin and around her face with an extra fold across the forehead, and suddenly she became orthodox. It was chilling to watch. I got goose bumps, and she shook it off as if she had ventured into frightening fashion territory.

I have friends in Turkey almost distraught at this country's movement to the right. Imagine not being fundamentalist and watching your country gradually become so – one universal interpretation of scripture, religious clothing and prayer in schools, women covering up and accepting a scripturally ordained subservient role to men, laws being rewritten. Imagine a ruling class that believes God is on its side – and others are wrong.

That night I went out without our crew for dinner. I felt a need to be alone in Istanbul. On the street level, the restaurant I had chosen was dead – but a TV monitor was showing the action up on the terrace, four flights up. I climbed the steps and sat down to dinner with the domes of the Blue Mosque on one side of me; on the other side, freighters were patiently waiting their turn to slip through the bottleneck of the Bosphorus. My dinner grace was forced on me as calls to prayer rang out from the minarets of neighborhood mosques all around. It was surround-sound: *Allahu Akbar* – 'God is great.'

I was gazing at the Christmas-tree lights that draped the minarets spiking into the sky above my dinner table, when suddenly the waiter's face filled my view, and he plopped down a hot, fresh-out-of-the-oven loaf, a pillow-shaped balloon of bread.

After dinner, I walked home the long way, savoring the Istanbul night. A local couple was sucking on a four-foot-tall hookah while cuddled up on one of the sofas that are so common these days in outdoor lounges. The pair seemed lost in each other's gaga eyes.

I stepped into the Blue Mosque, as if to give it another chance. Earlier it had been flooded with cruise-ship visitors. Now it was just the neighborhood mosque in action – not a tourist in sight. A window was open for ventilation. I peeked through to find it was the prayer zone for women. I drew back, suddenly feeling a tinge of Peeping Tom guilt.

A family gathered around their little boy in his proud admiral's outfit. It was his circumcision party – celebrated as Christians would celebrate a baptism, but even more joyously. (Turks call the circumcision party the greatest celebration – like 'a wedding without the in-laws.') The boy was all smiles ... for now.

Looking up, I enjoyed a treat that sneaks up on me whenever I find myself at mosques after dark: the sight of soaring birds with floodlit undersides, pumping hard in the humid Mediterranean air, swooping past silhouetted minarets.

Leaving the mosque, I came upon a big electronic readerboard. It was evangelizing, constantly spooling out delightful, Mohammad-praising, 'love-thy-neighbor' aphorisms in crawling red letters. After a few minutes pondering the verses, I thought, 'Good religious marketing.'

Just outside the gate, a man was drawing tourists' names on plates, mesmerizing a small crowd with his gorgeous calligraphy. While Western tourists in Turkey tend to assume that anyone 'foreign-looking' is a local, I've realized that in Istanbul's tourist zones, many of the 'exotic locals' are actually visitors from other parts of the Islamic world.

My day's little victory lap was just about done. Tourists filled a big patio, enjoying a single dervish whirling on an elevated platform. I have a bad attitude towards dervishes whirling for Westerners who have no idea what's going on, because I've enjoyed the good fortune of having a dervish actually explain the meaning of this meditational prayer ritual. But I buried my negativity and simply enjoyed the beauty of his performance, there in the Istanbul night.

I headed back to my hotel, climbed into bed, and started reviewing the memories generated by simply spending a few minutes walking around the block after dinner in Istanbul. It affirmed my love of this city, which I rank (along with Paris, Rome, and London) as one of Europe's greatest.

I thought back to one of my favorite shots from our day of filming. When the sun was low and the chop of the Bosphorus carbonated the scene, I stepped onto a dock. Behind me, a frilly mosque softened the harsh lines created by the mighty Bosphorus Bridge as it connected Asia and Europe. Just as a ship entered the frame, I looked into the lens and said, 'Like its mighty intercontinental bridge, Istanbul brings East and West together. With a complex weave of modern affluence, Western secularism, and traditional Muslim faith, it's a dynamic and stimulating city, well worth a visit.'

A Shaggy Dog Tale

EILIS KIRWAN

Eilis Kirwan is an Irish screenwriter and filmmaker. Her first produced screenplay, shot in Romania, is *The Whistleblower,* starring Rachel Weisz, Vanessa Redgrave, Monica Bellucci, and David Strathairn. She lives in Los Angeles, where she was recently stopped by someone asking if her dog has representation. They are considering their options.

A Shaggy Dog Tale

This journey starts and ends in Los Angeles, stopping off in New York, Frankfurt, Bucharest, Geneva, Munich and Paris. It demands intricate strategizing, the implantation of digital microchips, special immunizations, and the procurement of papers for crossing numerous international borders. From a dawn passage through Romanian airport customs to a late-night drive across the French–Swiss border, no effort is spared to overcome the obstacles. Is this the plot of the international political thriller I have written, inspired by true events, which is about to be filmed, after seven years of rewrites and hustle? No. It's the story of what it took to get myself and my dog to Romania for the duration of the shoot.

Perhaps I should double-back for some context. This is a shaggy dog tale. Not only because the preparations and the journey are more absurd and diverting, like most things in life, than the arrival. But also because it is the tale of a shaggy mutt named Ellie. This is no teacup accessory dog in a Louis Vuitton bag, but a blonde, smiley, Muppet-faced terrier rescued from the mean streets of Los Angeles. She has been with us a year, was clearly abused in her previous life, and is still in the tentative process of trusting her new family. Now we're off to Romania for two months. I don't want to break that trust.

It's worth noting that, up to this point in my life, while I have had the luck to travel widely, I have done so by the seat of my pants: booking at the last minute, packing at two in the morning, running for planes, sitting delirious in the cabin with no itinerary or accommodation arranged at the other end. I have not had to factor in anything beyond my own needs. I would arrive, bleary-eyed, in Sydney, Delhi or Bangkok, greeted by unfamiliar light and a host of unconsidered options. This resulted in a mix of great discoveries, close scrapes, and everything in between. It was part of the adventure. But that was then. Now I have a travel companion who needs special treatment and who can't just buy a seat. It's the beginning of a process that will change me from the slapdash flake of yore to an ultra-prepared traveling machine and something of a dog whisperer.

I am determined not to bring the dog if plane travel is going to be more stress than she can handle. Because of the past abuse, Ellie is still a nervous dog, wary of the unknown. I elicit advice from anyone who'll listen, waylaying dog owners on the street, in the dog park, the pet store. I trawl the internet for dog travel tales. In the end the vet assures me that the dog will be happier to be with me than to stay with friends who go out to work every day. She's used to life with a stay-at-home screenwriter. But there's one last check: is she small enough to be accepted for travel in the cabin? I measure and weigh her. She's within the regulations of most airlines, but only just. She can't afford to gain a pound. And she needs to be able to turn around in the carrier. I buy the standard-issue Sherpa dog carrier and take it home to test. I throw treats in. She gets in. She fits. I throw treats in the other end. She turns around. We're in business. Then she swiftly jumps out. Okay, it's going to take some practice. But the decision is made and there's no turning back. I will be the crazy lady who takes her dog to the movie set.

Now to procure the equivalent of a dog passport. Every country has unique regulations involving the 'importation of animals.' Most require an implanted microchip, proof of vaccination, and a blood test certificate. The process of chipping Ellie (to make her identifiable by European digital scanners) and blood-testing her (to prove she is vaccinated against rabies) takes a month-and-a-half, including detours. When a microchip implant goes AWOL in her body, literally lost in her ass, we have to redo the whole process. I will need veterinary certificates in different languages. The lab report. Multiple copies of each.

I am suddenly a tenacious, nitpicky stickler for detail and paperwork. Ellie and I become well known to the terrific staff of the Glendale Small Animal Hospital, who, I fear, roll their eyes when I leave. I am on first-name terms with the staff of the Rabies Laboratory at Kansas State University and everyone at the USDA office for animal transport in Hawthorne. I am determined to get this right. The regulations on official websites read tough and uncompromising. I do not want the dog to be detained at customs or taken into quarantine because of any omission on my part. I do not want to make her feel as unsafe as she did in her earlier life. I also have to get to the movie set urgently. Throughout this whole process I am doing production rewrites, double-checking research on the true story our script is inspired by, and communicating with my cowriter, who is also the director. That is my full-time day job. But my personal project, my labor of love, is all dog.

We know she fits in the Sherpa bag. But will she stay in it? Will she bark and whine? Can she sit still for hours on end? The vet tells me that he can give me tranquilizers but doesn't advise using them unless the dog has a total meltdown because they can result, at best, in the dog getting agitated or, at worst, in ... respiratory failure and death. Needless to say, unless Ellie goes so postal that she leaps out of the Sherpa bag with a shoulder-mounted missile launcher aimed at myself and the other passengers, I won't be using tranquilizers. So we're going to have to plan.

That means training. Ellie knows how to sit on command. But I want her to learn to get 'down' in the carrier bag, and to stay even if it's open. So we spend time every morning and evening practicing. I tempt her with treats, luring her to the ground, teaching the word 'down.' She starts getting it. We repeat it over and over. It's the training montage from Rocky. I'm hearing those trumpets in my head. Imagining Ellie ascending the iconic steps in Philadelphia.

She's a fast learner. Soon enough she's up and down like a champion sheepdog, and it's time for test runs. My strategy is to exhaust her with fun and frolics, then take her for acclimating trips. We take long hikes, then go on night drives all over Los Angeles. We coast down Sunset, me driving, her in the carrier on the passenger seat, gradually upping each journey's duration. Ten minutes around the neighborhood and home. Then twenty, thirty, ever increasing ... Finally we cruise all the way from Echo Park to Santa Monica, smooth music on the stereo. I chat away in a soothing voice. Yes, I am losing my mind, but we will be ready. And at this point, she's chilling, lying back in the womb-like comfort of that carrier and settling in for the ride. I'm not sure anymore if these test runs are for her or for me. But it's working.

The date of our departure arrives. We rise early and go for a long hike. I fine-tune our packing, which was done over a week ago, feed her no later than four hours before the flight, and we take another long walk. I make sure she relieves herself over and over. I have chosen Lufthansa for its generous regulations in terms of dog size and space under the seat for the carrier. Our first stop is New York, where we'll overnight at a friend's place. I'm breaking the journey into manageable parts and taking night flights to avoid the wafts of food that a dinner service would bring. The red-eye also mimics the sensation and duration of a night's sleep. This will apply to the dog but not to me, who will remain wide awake the whole flight, checking on her every five minutes. We are not supposed to open the carrier, but I reach in to keep her calm during take-off and landing. Her brown eyes glint up at me in the darkness, and later when everyone is sleeping, I let her peek out, and stretch her legs. If the flight attendants notice, they pretend not to.

In New York we hang out with friends until our flight that night. Ellie eats early and we go for multiple walks. We play ball in a park by the Hudson as dusk falls and a sharp wind whips in off the river. We are faster pals now than we ever were before. All my neurosis about getting this right has been answered by her cooperation at every turn. She has gone from a scrawny, nervous street dog who would bark at any approaching stranger, to a loyal and sweet travel companion.

That night in security at JFK, Ellie in my arms as we go through the metal detector, we draw the attention of a stern-faced security guard. I'm scared he's guessed she's on the cusp of the weight barrier. Or he suspects I'm using her to smuggle some capsule of insidious material. He marches over, then, beaming, launches into questions about her breed, patting her, telling me about his dogs at home. She's meant to stay in the carrier, but he encourages me to let her out of the bag until the flight and foists 'supplies' on me: rubber gloves I presume are meant for more sinister purposes, but in this case to clean up any potential 'accidents.' I am taken aback by his warmth. Amid so many rules and regulations, a sympathetic human face is a surprise. When so much of plane travel has become an irritation or worse, a paranoid nightmare, this is a revelation to me, and I have Ellie to thank. Still, I flash her paperwork at anyone who'll look at it, but so far nobody's interested. After everything I've been through to get this stuff, I feel like Victor Laszlo with the letters of transit, and I plan to use them.

The flight to Frankfurt goes without a hitch. Ellie is completely relaxed. I still watch her like a hawk for the seven-hour flight. We have a short wait in Frankfurt airport, made easier by the Germans' dog friendliness. Unlike most airports, here dogs are allowed out of the carrier so long as they are on leash. I take the chance to let Ellie stretch her legs and we even manage to have a bite and play. Then it's the final leg for Bucharest. As we fly the couple of hours left of our long journey, I wonder what will greet us when we get there. I have a lot of work ahead of me. But first, we have to get through customs.

Landing in Bucharest, Romania, I prep all the documentation, sure they'll give us a run for our money at customs. I have encountered post-Soviet bureaucracy on a research trip for this movie and it ranged from awkward to totally obstructive. It's early. A gray morning fills up with white light. When we disembark, the airport is empty and quiet. I collect my luggage, then peer into the customs area. I case the space, looking for European-issue animal scanners, hoping Ellie's microchip has not gone AWOL in her body again. I search for weighing scales, for ex-KGB customs agents who will aggressively inspect our papers. We slowly approach the area, my heart beating, and ... breeze through, Ellie's head sticking up out of the bag. Out in the arrivals area I search for information desks, the 'animal import' department, the police ... Don't they need to stamp Ellie's papers, validate them ... validate me? I don't want trouble later. Women behind desks shrug as I flash Ellie's letters of transit. Nobody cares.

A car takes us to the Hilton in the center of Bucharest, just around the corner from Revolution Square, where the 1989 revolution began. Faced with evidence of historic struggles, I fear the Romanian crew will think I'm a frivolous Hollywood tool bringing my dog all the way from LA. I drop my stuff at the hotel and we are taken straight to the set, located at a studio in Buftea, about twelve miles outside Bucharest. Upon arrival in Buftea, my fears are dispelled. The studio grounds teem with tens, perhaps hundreds of dogs – stray but tame, wild but an accepted part of life. Later, when I see more of Bucharest, I will learn this is a citywide phenomenon. So much so that, I am told, when the government moved to round up the stray dogs, not to euthanize but neuter them, uproar among the people put a stop to it. This explains the dogs and puppies at the studio – toddling through the offices, into the art department workshop, hanging around doorways.

Bucharest is dog heaven. Food scraps are thrown onto the street for dogs daily. Ellie meets movie stars, rests in the trailer while I work, and socializes with the local mutts. Standing on a night shoot in the Romanian countryside, mist floating in off the lake onto the set, I eye Ellie curled up in the director's chair under a warm heat lamp. And I know I made the right decision. She's having a great time. In a different way, so am I. I'm working hard, rewriting material for the realities of a tightly budgeted indie production. I'm seeing a script I've written produced for the first time. In between I take the dog for walks around Bucharest: past Revolution Square, up to Izvor or Cişmigiu Park. We play ball with Ceauşescu's gargantuan palace looming in the background. When I can't manage it, a young German woman named Gesa, here to mind the production designer's toddler and to get some experience on a movie set, takes on the dog. Despite the stress and pressure of the production, there is a shared, passionate drive to get this story told, and an amazing sense of everyone pitching in, even down to the welfare of a shaggy dog. Six weeks later, we've got it in the can.

It's time to go home. En route we will visit new friends in Geneva and Burgundy, driving late at night over French and Swiss borders where, once again, nobody is bothered about the papers we worked so hard to get. We are experts now, and the travel is smooth. We fly our favorite, Lufthansa, which means stopovers in Paris and one last overnight stop in Munich to allow time for the dog to eat, relieve herself, and exercise. We stay adjacent to the airport. We will catch our flight home the next morning (my preferred overnight flights are a no-go in this direction). In order to fulfill my strategy of making sure Ellie eats no later than four hours before flying and to ensure enough exercise to make her calm in the carrier, I have to rise at three in the morning. We walk through the empty streets of this Munich suburb, as snow twists in a silent breeze. We pass shuttered stores, restaurants, and homes. It's so peaceful, so serene. I imagine us home in Los Angeles tomorrow, where the sun will warm us, and the orange tree outside our front door will be fragrant and full of fruit. I try a quick 'down' with Ellie. She hunkers calmly. I walk away from her on the empty road, saying, 'Stay.' She doesn't move, and watches me confidently with her big, dark eyes. Snow dances between us like orange blossoms. It wasn't easy but here we are, one last ride from home, our trust not only unbroken, but rock solid. This journey has changed us both. I pat her, pick up the leash, and we turn and head for home.

Showdown in Real de Catorce

BOB BALABAN

Bob Balaban has appeared in about a hundred movies, including *Midnight Cowboy, Close Encounters of the Third Kind* and *Waiting for Guffman*. He produced and co-starred in *Gosford Park,* which won Academy, Bafta and Screen Actors Guild Awards, and directed *Bernard and Doris* and *Georgia O'Keeffe* for television, both of which were nominated for Emmy, Golden Globe, Screen Actors Guild and Directors Guild of America Awards. He wrote a bestselling series of children's books called *McGrowl* (Scholastic) and is currently writing a new series for Viking called *The Creature from the Seventh Grade*. His most recent film appearance is in Wes Anderson's movie *Moonrise Kingdom*.

It's 1998. Sometime in April. My agent calls and tells me there's interest in me playing the villain in *The Mexican,* a new Julia Roberts/Brad Pitt movie for DreamWorks. It starts shooting in six weeks in Los Angeles and Mexico. Gore Verbinski is directing. He made a movie I like a lot called *Mouse Hunt* (and has since directed the *Pirates of the Caribbean* franchise). He and the producer, Lawrence Bender *(Reservoir Dogs, Pulp Fiction, Kill Bill)*, are in LA. I'm in New York, and can't come in to meet them. I tell my agent I'll put myself on tape.

I get out the family video camera (this is pre-videophones) and ask my twelve-year-old daughter to film me reading a couple of scenes from the movie in my living room. I tell her to try not to jiggle the camera too much, and to zoom in and out a few times. The whole thing takes about five minutes. I send in the tape and forget about it. Much to my surprise, a few days later I get the job and before I know it I am on a plane to Los Angeles to shoot some interiors. Filming in LA goes well, and soon I am on my way to San Luis Potosí, Mexico, the closest city with an airport within 500 miles of our location, Real de Catorce.

After my five days of shooting in Mexico, my part will be wrapped and I will be homeward bound. Which is a good thing because I've got to get back to New York in two weeks to see my older daughter graduate from Sarah Lawrence. It looks like I'll be there in plenty of time. The movie gods are already laughing as we begin our descent into the middle of what looks like the Sahara Desert, only bigger.

It's easy to spot my driver in San Luis Potosí's tiny airport. Of the six people in baggage claim he's the only one who isn't wearing sandals and a sombrero and carrying a rifle. It's hot.

And I'm already thirsty. We get into our limousine and begin the six-hour schlep over winding dirt roads to the location.

'Real de Catorce is over 10,000 feet above sea level,' my driver explains. 'Staying hydrated is one of the best ways to avoid altitude sickness.' He hands me a bottle, which I'm not drinking because it says 'bottled in Mexico' in small print on the bottom of the label and I'm no dummy.

He also warns me that I may feel a little tired until I get acclimated. 'Get plenty of rest,' he advises. 'And stay away from the scorpions. They're everywhere.'

He fails to mention you also have to stay away from the food and the blistering sun that will fry you to a crispy burnt sienna in less than five minutes of exposure to the famously thin mountain air.

On the way I read a pamphlet I picked up in the airport. 'The town of Real de Catorce, population less than a thousand' – take it from me, a lot less – 'was once a thriving silver mining settlement. It has long been a pilgrimage site for both local Catholics and Huichol shamanists, and is now being discovered by tourists drawn by the desert ambience and its reputed spiritual energy.

'Enrico Caruso sang here regularly in the city's lavish opera house, and an international group of cosmopolitan travelers, ex-patriots and mine owners from across the globe frequented the local bullring, a number of quaint but lovely hotels, and shops featuring the finest in European luxury goods.' Sounds promising. 'In 1900, when the price of silver plummeted, Real de Catorce was all but abandoned and remains the "ghost" town you see today.' Make that 'sounded' promising.

'From the main road you will traverse a seventeen-mile-long cobblestone path ... until you reach the 1.5-mile-long Ogarrio Tunnel, which only accepts vehicles one way, with travelers in and out having to wait their turn.'

Wait. It gets worse. What the pamphlet fails to mention is that until the movie began prepping the location nearly two months ago, the tunnel had no electricity whatsoever, and several hapless backpackers who happened to find themselves wandering through, dropped briskly into open mineshafts and were never heard from again.

At this point my mouth is so dry that my tongue is like cardboard, and I am so car-sick that I have to put my pamphlet down and stare straight ahead to avoid throwing up. As we enter the tunnel we are plunged into sudden darkness, until our eyes become accustomed to the light from a few randomly spaced 25-watt light bulbs dangling from the roof of the tunnel, which provide sufficient illumination to keep us from crashing into a wall. But as far as anything requiring actual 'vision,' like avoiding a coyote, or a boulder, or god forbid an open mineshaft. Let's just say we're on our own.

After what feels like days, I am safely deposited at last, weak and shaky, in the middle of the picturesque, though dusty, town square. Whatever time and wind and heat and dust can erase, they have. A few burros wander around aimlessly looking for water, as I drag my bag a few hundred yards up what might have been a charming, rose-covered, delicately winding path when Caruso was here, but would now be best described as a steep and barren, rock-strewn breeding ground for scorpions and tarantulas.

Halfway up the hill, I stop and massage the cramp in my side until I catch my breath, my head clears and I recover enough strength to make it to the entrance of a small pueblo-like structure carved deep into the side of the mountain. This will be home for the next ten days. A quick perusal reveals a few chairs, a side table, and a threadbare oriental carpet. A large overhead electric fan rotates slowly and ineffectively. It is not hard to believe that some scenes from *The Treasure of the*

Sierra Madre were actually filmed in this place. It is, however, hard to believe that travelers, however cosmopolitan, ever considered it lovely. Or quaint. Or even a hotel.

The first thing I do after I am deposited in my room is search for scorpions and tarantulas. I look in the corners of the closet, under the bed, and in the bathtub. I shake out all towels (which would be my hiding place of choice if I were a poisonous arachnid). So far so good. I go to what passes for the lobby to get an extra bath mat, and run into the crew for the electronic press kit (EPK) who will be shooting interviews with us for the DVD. They tell me about this great Italian restaurant run by some expats a few hills down from the hill on which we are staying. I ask if it is safe to eat the food there and they assure me it is perfectly fine. Everything is flown in from southern California. Or Texas. Or somewhere.

I eat a great Italian meal. I'm not kidding. I drink Coca-Cola bottled in the good old USA, and scarf down the best gnocchi with truffles I have had in a long time. By the time I am back in my room fully sated, I am somewhat used to the altitude and eager to get a good night's sleep. I carefully search every inch of my covers for animal life, and finding none, drift quickly off to sleep. It's like Stanley Kubrick directed my dreams. All night long I soar through jungles populated by red elephants and flying glass monkeys. When I finally awaken I remember the driver saying something about altitude-induced 'nightmares.' Boy was he right. I shower, careful to shake out my towel, and after I examine my clothing both inside and out, I check out my shoes for uninvited guests, get dressed and try to go to work.

You would think it wouldn't be hard to find a crew of 150 alligator-shirted Angelinos shooting a movie with Julia Roberts and Brad Pitt in the middle of a town in Mexico the size of a Kmart. But it takes me a few minutes before I realize that the crew and the actors are all hiding behind a large black curtain as big as a small mountain that has been erected to protect everyone from the hoard of paparazzi who have assembled to try to snap the first photo of Brad Pitt and Julia Roberts 'together' in the history of paparazzi-dom.

Dozens of photographers have been flooding the tiny village since someone who saw Julia and Brad arrive at the airport tipped off someone who tipped off someone who put it all over the internet. It's a feeding frenzy. Both actors stay close to their hotel-like quarters, and have their meals cooked for them 'in house.'

The next few days drift by in a hazy fog of filming, as I try to avoid getting terminal food poisoning, or bitten by a scorpion or a tarantula, or altitude sickness. While remembering my lines.

>>>>>>>>>>>>>>>>

The script supervisor is toweling off after a shower and gets stung by a scorpion. Fortunately it's just a baby scorpion, so she only gets numb and weak for a little while, and will be able to go back to work in a few days after her blurry vision gets better and the antidote takes full effect. I promise you, if it had been me, I'd have been medevaced home yesterday.

>>>>>>>>>>>>>>>>

I don't see the EPK crew anywhere. An assistant director tells me that after last night's dinner (in the same restaurant where I had my delicious gnocchi) they came down with such violent *turista* they are all sequestered in their pueblo and may have to be sent to the nearest hospital 200 miles away.

>>>>>>>>>>>>>>>>

My character gets shot in the neck by Julia, and I get to have fake blood spurt out of a prosthetic device and fall backward out of the shot onto pillows. The gun goes off. The blood spurts. I fall like a professional. It's my favorite death scene.

>>>>>>>>>>>>>>>>

While walking across the town square I encounter three confused young hippy tourists passing through town, which is the polite way of saying that three peyote-ridden addicts hoping to get even higher on the vibes from the little village's reputed 'spiritual energy' are having a super-bad trip.

These guys are totally wasted. They have been drugging for days as they made it through the surrounding desert. How they managed to avoid falling into a mineshaft when skipping through the Ogarrio Tunnel I will never know. But here they are, and something terrible must have just happened to them because they are looking into the sun and taking off their shades and blinking and stammering, 'Oh, man, oh jeez, oh man,' like they have just seen the mother ship landing.

'Hey mister,' they call when they see me. 'Where are we? What's going on?' Clearly something has freaked them out.

'What's the matter?' I ask politely, being sure to stay back a few feet in case one of them has a sudden LSD flashblack and turns violent.

'We just saw ... oh man,' one of the guys says. 'You tell him, Janie. I can't. It's too weird.'

'We think we just saw Julia Roberts and Brad Pitt walk by,' their young Janis Joplin–like friend tells me. 'And we're worried we're overdosing. Can you tell us what's really happening?'

I patiently explain that they really did see Julia and Brad. And that they have stumbled across a $60 million movie being filmed in the middle of their hallucination-filled camping trip to a spiritual mecca in the middle of Nowhere with a capital 'N.' I am still not sure whether or not they believed me. They hung around for a few hours. Watched the big black velveteen curtain for a while. And then got bored and wandered back through the tunnel of death.

>>>>>>>>>>>>>>>

The paparazzi are getting so aggressive that one of them tries to tear down the black wall of Jericho and storm the set, so Brad and Julia's publicist comes up with a brilliant plan: Julia's friend is going to take a million pictures of the two of them posing together, sell them all over the place, and devalue their worth. The minute the paparazzi learn of this devilish plan they evaporate back into the desert quicker than a mirage. And we are bothered no more.

>>>>>>>>>>>>>>>

So now it's my fifth day of filming in Real de Catorce and if all goes well I will be on the plane back to New York tomorrow morning. I call home, relieved to inform my family that the movie is on schedule. The weather is fine. And I will be there in plenty of time to witness the momentous occasion of my daughter's graduation.

And then, of course, everything falls apart. First they have to reshoot a scene they did before I even got here because the negative got scratched. Okay. We're only a day behind. I'll still make it.

And then the weather starts to change. All of a sudden it's cold and cloudy in the middle of this arid desert that hasn't seen weather like this in about 200 years. We are shooting the climactic scene at the end of the movie and waiting for the sun to come out. It is five in the afternoon. Brad races off to change into the costume he must wear in case the sun really does make a brief appearance.

And then it actually does peep out for about a minute. It's perfect. The sky turns golden. You can see the rainbow forming in the distance. The shot will be amazing. Someone runs to get Brad in his pueblo – but they can't find him because all the pueblos look exactly alike. Then they do locate him and just as he races back, panting and tucking in his shirt tails and trying to catch his breath (even movie stars have trouble with altitude, not just me), the sun goes back behind its cloud and it starts to pour. Add one more scene to our day's work.

Even I can see at this point where this is all headed. And so, I assume, can you.

Eventually my family forgave me. They knew how hard I tried. And how upset I was when I finally got back fifteen hours too late. And they may even forget eventually. But I never will. The moral of my story is simple.

Your pitfall may arise whence you least expect it. And hit you harder than a case of Asian flu. So travel with care, fellow readers, and take my lesson to heart. You must never depend upon the weather to do what you need it to do. And if someone you truly care about is expecting you to attend an important event at the end of your trip? You better stay home. As my cousin Fanny always used to say: you cannot ride two horses with one ass. And you are a fool if you think you can.

With two burros it's even harder.

Trust me. I was there.

Shooting in Romania: What Doesn't Kill You ...

PAULINA PORIZKOVA

International supermodel Paulina Porizkova has graced the covers of magazines worldwide for more than a decade. She began modeling at the age of fifteen and quickly rose to the top of her profession. Paulina's acting life began with the title role in *Anna*. She has also appeared in *Her Alibi, Arizona Dreams, Female Perversions, Thursday* and sixteen other films. In the past two years, she has written about beauty and its cost for the *Huffington Post* and *Modelinia*. Her recent television appearances include *The Oprah Winfrey Show,* multiple appearances on CNN's *Parker Spitzer, The Joy Behar Show* and *The Late, Late Show with Craig Ferguson*. Paulina has also written a novel, *A Model Summer,* and a children's book, *The Adventures of Ralphie the Roach*. She lives with her family in New York City.

When, in the year 2000, I was offered the starring part in a horror-adventure flick co-starring Judd Nelson and Larry Drake, there was really no reason for me to turn it down. I had two small kids, no career to speak of and was slowly going brain-dead. An offer to play a dead hooker would have seemed alluring. And this one was a starring part. So what kept me from jumping for joy and landing on the set? The movie was to be shot in Romania.

Now, I had been in a movie shot in Bisbee, Arizona, where the best, and only, restaurant was a Taco Bell. My hotel room had unmatched sheets with little trucks printed on them. Forms of entertainment were few; on our days off, we'd drive into the desert and shoot holes in our cowboy boots. I have also done several super-low-budget movies where I used my own clothes and changed behind a van, which also served as our equipment truck, makeup room, dressing room and cafeteria. So what was the big deal?

I had been to Romania before. It was beautiful. It was also one of the few countries in Eastern Europe that didn't fully adhere to the communist doctrine of 'all peoples should be equal and have equal food, or lack thereof.' Instead they had a rather confusing system, which blended the worst part of a communist regime with a dictatorship. Shooting a film there would make a super-low-budget film in the States look like the set of *Cleopatra*.

But the film's charming director and its charming producer assured me that Romania had changed. In the year 2000, ten years after Ceauşescu's reign of terror, Romania was ready to join Europe as a little sister rather than a hobo. A four-star hotel had been built in Bucharest (four stars as counted by Americans), where we were to stay. We were to shoot in the best television and movie studio in the country. I would be treated like the star I thought I deserved to be.

I knew enough to be skeptical; my children and husband stayed at home, just in case the reality was more like what I remembered.

After the super-luxury of Swissair first class, landing in Romania's airport and entering the smoke-filled and cigarette butt-laden luggage retrieval to meet my leathered, toothless taxi driver, I knew it was time to change my vision.

You see, I have two sets of eyes. Until the age of ten I was growing up in a place where no hot running water was the norm. The bathtub was tin, and carried to the kitchen, and baths were rationed to one a week. Heating came from coal stoves. Food poisoning was also a weekly occurrence, since we had no fridge or icebox. A banana was so sought after and rare that we only got one, and I mean one, for Christmas.

If this sounds like turn-of-the-century America, be aware that I'm not that old! Rather, I was born in the then communist Czechoslovakia. The benefits – besides being rather bacteria resistant – are these two sets of eyes I can switch between. With one set, my communist eyes, dirt and deprivation are familiar, and in no way hamper a good time. With the other, my capitalist set of eyes, anywhere you are not offered a hot towellete while reclining with a glass of champagne is uncivilized. All right, that's a bit of an exaggeration, but hot water and toilet paper are not optional.

This double vision comes in handy when traveling: I have no problems adjusting to whatever is at hand, unlike my single-pair-eyed family and friends. But generally I stick a pair of eyes on and leave them there until it's time to leave. Romania was to be different.

The first switch was the drive from the luxury hotel to the ancient Communist-regime television studio. It had an undeserved reputation as the best studio in the country, since it was the only one in the country. The road was paved for a good half of the way, but even on the paved parts, my tiny Mercedes and uniformed driver were often stuck behind a horse-and-carriage driven by an ancient weather-beaten man or an ancient toothless crone in a *babushka*. Thin, poorly dressed Roma children lined some parts of the road, hands outstretched, at the ungodly hours of four or five o'clock in the morning. Judd Nelson, my co-star, stopped every time, giving away all of his per diem in the first two days.

At night, we visited a gilt-dripping casino with all the accoutrements of Las Vegas, and walked back to our hotel through streets lined with buildings that still showed the bullet holes of the revolution that had deposed and executed Ceauşescu ten years earlier. The worst part of taking a walk thought the city, though, were the dogs – hordes of semi-wild, mangy, hungry, desperate dogs.

It was at some point explained to us that Ceauşescu had, towards the end of his reign, forcibly ejected thousands of people from their homes to build nicer looking buildings, without much caring where the evicted folks would go. I guess they went somewhere, since I didn't see too many homeless people, but they left their dogs to fend for themselves. Some of these homeless dogs went feral and chased us with growls and snarls from what they considered 'their' corners, but some wagged their tails and follow us for blocks. Some just lay there, so sick and hungry they exhausted themselves with the effort of lifting their heads when you passed. Even if you weren't an animal lover, it would still break your heart to see a four-week-old puppy dying between the paws of its mother, who'd nudge it toward you in a last attempt to save her baby. And if you wanted to rescue it, there were at least five more within the same block. Judd, Larry and I stopped taking walks.

At the studio, a perfect example of communist modern – blocky and gray – Judd, Larry and I were treated as first-class stars with giant dressing rooms and a private chef, and a dining room only for us and the director and producer. Only I, however, appreciated the cuisine of boiled meats and white starch. Larry and Judd were busy wrapping their leftovers into napkins for the dogs. Our dressing rooms didn't have heating, but they were furnished with '50s-style furniture that would probably be worth some money in the States.

The crew was all Romanian, and most of them, except for the hair and makeup people, spoke little or no English. This may have accounted for some of the small misunderstandings (as they saw it), or life-threatening miscommunications (as Judd and Larry saw it).

The first day into the shooting, Judd turned to me and announced he had a feeling that to shoot an action flick in a Third World country was a really bad idea. We were filming scenes in which he and I were crawling through air ducts, escaping from a mental patient (played by Larry) bent on killing us both. The second time Judd ripped his pants on a poorly welded seam, he was ready to call it a day and go back to the States. Safety on set didn't appear to be a priority.

With my communist vision, this seemed perfectly okay: people had done their jobs, so what if it wasn't perfect? You'd be insulting them if you pointed out the flaws.

This way of looking at things held true as long as the safety in question was Judd's pants. When we shot a scene in which the killer hurls himself through a glass window at me, a real glass window (the stuntman cut his head in five places), and I ended up with a face full of shattered glass, I started to feel more American. When, right before we were to do an explosion scene in the hallway, someone cleaned the floors with gasoline, my laughter was forced. (Judd was the one to call it; I thought the smell of gasoline came from the explosives.)

Then of course, there was the scene when my character, Maggie, finally makes it out of the asylum, which we shot outside the local morgue at night. Maggie has set an explosive at the massive doors and blown them off their hinges, and stumbles out through the smoke to the waiting police car. The smoke was made in two metal barrels right next to where I had to wait and make myself hyperventilate for the scene before bursting out, and it smelled suspiciously like burning plastic shopping bags. Which is exactly what it was. If I ever get lung cancer or emphysema later in my life, you'll never be able to convince me that it was caused by the cigarettes I've smoked.

One day we got lost on the way to our 'lunch', which was served in the lobby of the morgue in the middle of the night, and we accidentally walked through the actual morgue. The dead naked bodies stacked haphazardly on top of each other seemed a casual reminder of what happens when you ignore 'Safety First.'

My double vision was flicking on and off and on and off. It was enough to make me seasick. Or slightly schizophrenic. Ten minutes from my hotel, a Roma girl about six years old stood shivering barefoot on the roadside in November, holding her newborn sibling swathed in an old towel. Ten minutes in the other direction lived a beautiful clothing designer who owned a townhouse, all four stories gleaming with Lucite-lit flooring, expensive all-white furnishings reflected in huge mirrors and white mink throws sprinkled throughout. Her car outside was a white Cadillac Escalade with a television and video games, and of course, a white-uniformed driver. This was nothing like the communist country of my youth, but I wasn't sure I liked it any better.

My capitalist eyes demanded action. I realized I couldn't help one and leave all others, so I started to make plans for benefits and volunteer work I would do as soon as I got back home to the US. But with my communist eyes, the Roma kids and dying dogs were just a part of life. No need for action. This is how things went; you couldn't change it. You just coasted along the dirty waters as best you could until it was your time to go under. I guess this is why America is the most powerful nation on earth. In our American eyes there is nothing we can't do.

We finished the movie on schedule, my last scene being one in which my stuntwoman was to climb up a chain about three floors. Only just before we started filming this scene did we find out that my stuntwoman, or stunt girl, really, was not a stunt person at all, but just an actress. All the times she was jumping off roofs and elevator shafts and crashing through glass she was no more trained than I was.

I did the climbing myself. The first take became the only take, since after I brilliantly ascended to the ceiling, I had no strength to even hold a glass of water. But at least I did it. Until then I had no idea that I could climb three floors up a chain.

Shooting an action movie in Romania ended up being a bit like natural childbirth: the experience made you realize your strength.

I already knew I could float down a dirty stream and close my eyes to ugliness around me.

What I don't always remember, though, is how lucky I am that I don't have to.

Thai Dyed

ERIC BOGOSIAN

Eric Bogosian has starred in a number of feature films (including the adaptation of his play, *Talk Radio*) as well as playing Captain Dan Ross on *Law & Order: Criminal Intent* for three seasons. In addition to *Talk Radio*, Bogosian has written a number of plays, including *subUrbia* (which was also adapted to film), six solos shows and three novels. His latest novel, *Perforated Heart*, was published by Simon & Schuster last year.

I've filmed in Thailand twice. First in 1989 on a CBS Movie of the Week entitled *Last Flight Out* and then in '97 on an HBO movie, *Bright Shining Lie*. That second time we were put up in a Bangkok hotel for one night before shipping out to location. Despite being jet-lagged out of our skulls (a problem when location shooting halfway around the world), a bunch of us, including a Chinese-American actress in her late fifties, decided to go out and see the sights. We grabbed a cab in front of the hotel and asked the driver to take us someplace where we could see the sights. He chattered something back to us and off we roared toward Patpong, a popular tourist district packed with open-air bars and food stands and souvenir vendors. The driver arrived at a nondescript door, pointed and nodded, 'Ping-pong show, banana show, razorblade show?' He smiled beatifically. He'd wait.

What could this be? We headed for the door. In moments we figured out what the driver was describing. Oh yeah. Behind that door was the thing Patpong is most famous for, the sex show. We opted for dinner instead. We soon learned how ubiquitous the sex trade is in urban Thailand. But what's more impressive than the vast amount of carnal experiences available is the blasé attitude the locals seem to have toward the sex industry. Repeatedly I encountered completely innocent invitations to see strip shows or to employ prostitutes from really sweet hotel personnel. Of course, they recognized me as a Western male and simply assumed that's why I was in Thailand.

The learning curve would accelerate because we were shooting near the city of Pattaya, which is to the sex industry something like what Las Vegas is to gambling. Hanging out in Pattaya and not absorbing the predominant industry would be like going to the beach and not swimming. No visitor can avoid the bars that open onto the street. Prostitutes – young women, older women and young men in drag – lustily hail all who pass by. It's easy to see the roots of this once-tiny beach town when it was a Vietnam War–era R & R spot. After years of being the place where our boys in uniform relaxed, it grew and grew. Today it is a thriving, throbbing destination. How big? The Sixth Fleet was anchored there while we were shooting. That's something like 6000 sailors. Pattaya had no problem accommodating them.

Yes, I did visit a few places out of curiosity, but after two visits to go-go bars, I didn't return. I won't lie, there is something exciting about the demimonde of urban Thailand. It's impossible to erase the mental images of *The Deer Hunter*, which was shot there. But let's be clear: the sex industry is an adjunct to a hard and vicious crime world in Thailand. It is not cool or easygoing. The girls are very poor and for the most part sell intimacy because they are sending money back to their impoverished families. Some, if not most, are virtual slaves. After having a bar girl explain how her family sent her to the bars to make ten bucks a night, I lost my curiosity.

Thankfully, Pattaya is more than people selling their bodies and my most memorable night in Thailand was spent there. We finished work in the early evening and dispersed to find food. The sun had just set, which, due to the throbbing heat, is the cue to go out and about. We grabbed a túk-túk outside the hotel and roared into the city proper. There we found a wonderful theater that featured transvestite renditions of Broadway musicals. Just under the theater was a shooting gallery, where for five bucks one could grab a .45 or even a machine gun and blast away at targets. I wondered if the flooring between the range and the seating upstairs was bulletproof.

Having satisfied our artistic and martial needs, we ambled shoreward, where an open-air vendor displayed his freshly caught fish. The deal was that you picked out a fish you liked the look of, described how you'd like to have it cooked and then sat at a picnic table on the beach. Ten minutes later, I was served the best grilled fish with chili sauce I'd ever had.

Still, I was not in Thailand to play, but to work in-country. And it was here, on and around our sets, that I got to experience the real Thailand. I shared food with the Thai film crew (they had their own food service) and as a result will never again be satisfied with Americanized 'Thai' food. I visited village food stalls replete with fly-speckled slaughter, climbed multistory limestone waterfalls flitting with butterflies, was amazed and frightened by the immense night-time drone of jungle insect life, and in general had my entire sensory apparatus – taste, sight and smell – transported to new uncharted territory.

But the treasures of Thailand that brought me the most joy and satisfaction were the Buddhas in the temples. First and foremost was the massive reclining golden Buddha of Wat Pho in Bangkok. This wonderfully serene Buddha is 150-feet long, covered in gold and housed in a large airy shelter. I've been there a few times, I even have a little version of this Buddha over my desk to keep me company. Visiting temples became an addiction with me on both my trips. On my days off, I would simply ask my driver to find a Buddha. Because we were often in the jungle, getting there was half the fun.

The Buddhas of Thailand vary in quality and size. There have been instances of very small solid gold Buddhas found encased in large unremarkable plaster Buddhas. This was done in order to protect the inner, very valuable Buddha from pillage by conquering armies. I heard that one was discovered a few years back when a large plaster Buddha was dropped while being moved. It cracked in half to reveal the sacred solid gold deity within.

One day I found myself wandering around a monastery north of Kanchanaburi in Chiang Mai. The Buddha here was fat and ugly and poorly rendered. Disappointed, I was making my way back to the car park where my driver waited for me, when I passed a stand of incense and recognized it as a place to say a prayer and make a donation. So I did. Then I spied a little sign, in Thai, on the ground. Approaching it I saw that the sign indicated with an arrow an opening in the ground and a tiny ladder going down into the hole.

So I let myself down into the hole. At the bottom of the little ladder I found myself in a small limestone cave, maybe ten-feet wide. Here were some small Buddhas and more incense and candles. I let the vibes wash over me, alone in a cave underground. Then, like Alice, I noticed a small door, maybe three-feet high, set in the wall. It led into a little tunnel. In I went, noticing as I did that the little door had a loose padlock attached. I figured I wasn't going far, so I ignored the padlock.

That tunnel led to another cave. And another tunnel and another cave. And on and on. In each cave resided a Buddha. After three or four of these I remembered that padlock. Perhaps it would be a good idea to turn back. But I was curious: each succeeding cave was occupied by more interesting Buddhas! I couldn't stop now! The adrenaline flowed as I pressed on.

And then I had the great experience, what Spalding Gray called 'the perfect moment.' The last cave. High-ceilinged, spacious. With one wonderful supreme Buddha! No wonder the public Buddha outside was so crummy. He wasn't the real one, the significant one. He was the one for the tourists. This was the guy! Oh yeah. I hung there for a while, praying, thinking, alone who knows how many feet underground in a limestone cavern in Thailand.

Eventually I found my way out, found my driver and realizing the late hour, said, 'I better get back, production has no idea where I am. It's important.' He replied with classic Thai tranquility, 'Yes, yes, very important. I understand.'

The King and I

RICHARD E GRANT

Richard E Grant was born and brought up in Swaziland, emigrated to England in 1982, and since his first film *Withnail and I* in 1986, has appeared in forty films and worked with directors Francis Ford Coppola, Martin Scorsese, Jane Campion, Bruce Robinson and Robert Altman. Grant wrote and directed *Wah-Wah* in 2004. He has also published three books, *With Nails: The Film Diaries of Richard E Grant*, *The Wah-Wah Diaries: The Making of a Film* and *By Design: A Hollywood Novel*.

At the tail end of the last century, I scribbled an auto-biographical screenplay about my adolescence in Swaziland, Southern Africa, entitled *Wah-Wah* (the toodle-pip and hubbly-jubbly colonial slang of the last gasp of empire). After a couple of years trying to chicken-and-egg it – get it cast and financed – my producer politely withdrew to become a drugs counselor in Barbados. Into the breach stepped a comely French female producer (whom I shall diplomatically refer to by her initials, MC), who promised calm financial passage and clearsailingconditionsahead.com. Despite the invention of phones, faxes, texts and emails, the small matter of answering any of these communications between my office in London and hers in Paris became increasingly infrequent.

There's nothing like the hilarity of hindsight when revisiting the near nervous-breakdown-inducing details of working with the aforementioned foe ...

Having ploughed through four years of rewrites, preproduction collywobbles and yo-yoing financials, we finally find ourselves in Swaziland, only to discover, five days before shooting, that MC has 'neglected' to secure work permits for the hundred-plus crew and cast. She is still in Paris when I am red-carpeted by an incandescent Swazi government minister at 8:30am on June 2, 2004.

He detonates a full-frontal attack: 'WHERE ARE YOUR APPLICATIONS? WHY WAS THERE NO FOLLOW-UP? WHY WAS THERE NO CONTACT? WHERE WERE YOU, GRANT? WHY WERE YOU NOT HERE, GRANT? WHY WAS I NOT INFORMED, GRANT?'

He is unstoppable and implacable.

My feeble attempt to explain that the finances have collapsed and been resurrected, and the permits were the producer's responsibility, goes for a Burton. His voice is now two decibels below full shout. 'HIS MAJESTY IS ANGRY WITH YOU, THE CHIEF OF POLICE IS ANGRY WITH YOU, THE MINISTRY IS ANGRY WITH YOU. YOU CANNOT START FILMING IN FIVE DAYS' TIME!'

I plead, beg, explain and grovel – all to no avail.

'NO, NO, NO, NO, NO, NO, NO!'

In the poisonous silence that follows, all I can think about is what the response would be were a hundred foreigners to land at Heathrow or JFK airport without visas, permits or permissions of any description, intending to mosey down to Piccadilly Circus or Times Square for a two-month film shoot.

'We are completely at fault, sir, and I understand your position entirely. Thank you for meeting us so early in the morning and I deeply regret that we won't be able to make the film here or spend a large part of our budget in the kingdom.'

I know this is brinkmanship. There is no alternative. The likely reality is that it's all over before it's even properly begun. The minister says he will convene an emergency meeting and I should be on standby for his response.

Then I call Paris and, for once, manage to get straight through to MC, whose blood I am ready to boil.

'So you believe this minister? You believe him and not me?'

'That's not the fucking point! It doesn't matter who I believe. The point is we cannot start shooting because we do not have any work permits!'

'Go ask the king.'

How many times in the twenty-first century are you going to be asked to do this in real life? Her edict rattles around my cranium like a superannuated boiled sweet in tandem with 'You believe him and not me?' I cannot credit this insanity and start laughing. The notion that you could cajole a government minister in London, Washington, let alone Paris, to make an exception to these procedures at such short notice is plainly ludicrous.

The minister calls at 4:45pm and I am summonsed for a rundown of the demands: permits to be submitted first thing next day (minimum of a week to process), letters for location permissions to be delivered immediately, a substantial fine to be paid for the inconvenience. On and on it goes and all I can register is, 'This is a reprieve.'

He is at pains to point out that the film company has caused this delay, not the government, which is now expected to bend laws and make exceptions.

The production manager calls MC to report the results. Stunned silence.

Meanwhile in London, the actors are in a panic as they all have to report to a police station and get fingerprinted and pay for certificates to prove they're not ex-cons, which are then faxed to the Swazi government.

All we can hope for is to be granted an audience with the king to beg permission to start shooting on schedule whilst the applications are being processed.

At 9pm I get the call to be at the palace the next day.

At least the minister has not vetoed our chances of filming outright. Or so we think until we receive the license contract from the committee at 11am demanding an extra $20,000 on top of the $200,000 fee to cover 'administration, filming rights, policing, use of scenery etc,' plus a proviso that the film be vetted by the government before it is commercially released. Oh fuckity, fuckity, fuckity, fuck-fuck.

Four-and-a-half sphincter-winking hours drag by and then a call to 'Get to Lozitha Palace immediately.' We pile into the rental car and drive hell for leather. On the radio, Bob Marley is chanting 'Every little thing's gonna be alright' and we all hope that the man is right!

Royal protocol demands everyone is kept waiting for anything between one hour and eight to meet the king. The formerly incandescent minister has been waiting since noon. Does this mean the king has not yet heard his demands?

No sooner have we arrived at 3pm than we are ushered into the throne room, which ups our status instantly. The king, who I have met once a couple of years before, greets me with real warmth and insists that I sit beside him on a matching throne. As is Swazi custom, the minister sits shoeless before the monarch on the floor. Surreal.

'Your Majesty, we are asking for your blessing to let filming go ahead. We simply do not have an extra $200,000 as stipulated by the minister this morning.' The king's wide-eyed reaction confirms that this is the first time he has heard about this.

We are granted a royal reprieve. The power of an absolute monarch never seemed so sweet.

Postscript: *Wah-Wah* was released in 2006, the minister has since been fired and MC's company went into liquidation.

Behind the Scenes: Filming Tomb Raider at Angkor Wat

NICK RAY

As well as authoring more than thirty titles for Lonely Planet in destinations as diverse as Cambodia and Rwanda, Nick Ray has worked in television and film since the late 1990s. Following the success of *Lara Croft: Tomb Raider*, he has scouted locations for feature films such as Jean-Jacques Annaud's *Two Brothers*, and has worked with celebrities such as Charley Boorman, Jeremy Clarkson and Gordon Ramsay, introducing them to adventures, and some trouble, in remote parts of Cambodia, Laos and Vietnam.

Life doesn't always follow the script. The original call came from Oliver Stone. He was working on a film called *Beyond Borders,* a sort of *Dr Zhivago* of the NGO world, set to star Meg Ryan in the female lead. We spent two weeks scouting around Cambodia for potential locations for a Khmer refugee camp set on the Thai border in the 1980s before a fateful call arrived from the *Tomb Raider* crew.

As a postscript to the Oliver Stone experience, *Beyond Borders,* starring Angelina Jolie and Clive Owen, was eventually directed by Martin Campbell, and the Cambodia scenes were shot on a vacant housing site outside Chiang Mai, Thailand. But in the meantime, the *Tomb Raider* crew were keen to scout around Angkor. The original film script had the Terracotta Army coming to life, but a Chinese film had already featured this very story. Luckily for Cambodia, the art department team had a coffee-table book on Angkor and director Simon West was hooked. Clearly, it was meant to be and two weeks later we were scouring the temples of Angkor with the crew.

Tomb Raider was the first major Hollywood film to hit Cambodia since *Lord Jim,* starring Peter O'Toole, back in 1964. It was a major gamble for Paramount Pictures, as 20th Century Fox had been roundly condemned for its heavy-handed treatment of the coastline around Ko Phi Phi during the filming of *The Beach.* Everyone involved was determined that such dramas would not unfold at Angkor and so the preparations began.

My role as a location manager was to select the locations and work with the production team to secure the necessary permissions. It was a bureaucratic minefield. Cambodia was still governed by a coalition of the Cambodian People's Party (CPP), the former communists installed in power by the Vietnamese in 1979 after the Khmer Rouge defeat, and Funcinpec, a loose alliance of royalists who had spent much of the 1980s fighting the CPP from their bases in the refugee camps along the Thai border. Deciding which faction to work with was one of the most important calls on the whole shoot. In the end we went with the CPP as the real powerbrokers in Cambodia, the royal family being largely symbolic and their political influence on the wane.

First stop was the Ministry of Culture to arrange a general filming permission. Her Royal Highness Princess Norodom Bopha Devi was the Minister of Culture at this time and *Tomb Raider* didn't exactly sound like a culturally sensitive movie about Cambodia's national treasure, the sacred temples of Angkor. The approval process headed to the Council of Ministers, where line producer Kulikar Sotho was granted a fifteen-minute meeting to convince Deputy Prime Minister Sok An of the project's merits. It moved to the cabinet for debate and was passed fifteen to one in favor. We had the green light, everything was in place – but this was when things really started to get complicated.

The locations chose themselves, as Angkor has such an embarrassment of riches to offer. We settled on the mountain temple of Phnom Bakheng as an establisher for the temples, with Angelina Jolie scanning the horizon to find a way into the lost complex, a nice piece of CGI wizardry that saw the East Gate of Angkor Thom superimposed upon the Cambodian jungle. A compressor provided the wind in her hair and for once the sunset over Angkor Wat was not the headline act: the tourists were far more interested in looking at Angelina in her hot pants. The bad guys were already trying to break in through the front door by pulling down a giant polystyrene *apsara* statue that had been moulded into the archway of the East Gate. Angelina needed wheels so she picked up her 650-horsepower custom Land Rover Defender, whizzed around Bayon temple a few times for glorious effect, and set off to find the back door.

Wandering amid the tentacle-like tree roots of Ta Prohm, she eventually found a secret entrance, plucking a sprig of jasmine before falling through the earth into Pinewood Studios near Windsor. Here she and the bad guys did battle with a giant multi-armed Hindu god before she escaped her adversaries by diving off the 35-meter-high waterfall at Phnom Kulen. Eventually she found her way to the royal pond of Angkor Wat, complete with a fully fledged floating village that happened to be there on that particular day. She borrowed a mobile phone from a friendly monk and received a blessing, which miraculously healed her wounded arm. Cambodia's starring moment had come and gone – but what about the madness behind the scenes?

>>>>>>>>>>>>>>

The East Gate of Angkor Thom is also known as the Gate of the Dead to Khmers, as this is where the bodies of kings were taken from the city for ceremonial cremation. Local heritage police were contracted to guard the site at night, as containers and props littered the area. On the second day, they wanted to quit, convinced they had heard the armies of Jayavarman VII marching through the gate at night. The only way to placate them was to hold a *bon,* a traditional ceremony to appease the spirits. Chickens duly slaughtered, they were happy to continue in their duties.

The Cambodian jungle is lush and green, but November marks the start of the dry season. Clearly the Cambodian jungle wasn't quite lush enough for the *Tomb Raider* team, as they decided to decorate it with $2000 worth of tropical plants from the local garden centre. The problem was that without the guarantee of rain, the plants would need a daily dose of water. It was time to negotiate with the local fire brigade. The boys in red were only too glad for a piece of the action and a deal was struck for them to act as our gardeners.

They were so excited to be playing the part that they drove out to the set with sirens blaring and lights flashing. The road to East Gate is an ancient causeway and very narrow. The fire engine flew along with no apparent concern for the art department pick-up truck trundling along the other way. Just as a head-on collision looked inevitable, the fire engine swung sharply to the right, so sharply in fact that it tumbled off the causeway, rolled on to its side and buried itself in the jungle foliage. We were incensed by their recklessness, but the responsibility of rescuing the fire engine fell on the film crew as the contractors. It was the only working fire engine in town, so we were under real pressure to get it back on the road. A ten-ton crane and a grab truck managed the job between them, but it was 1am before the fire engine was back at the station. Amazingly enough, the firemen drove more cautiously in the subsequent weeks.

A major-feature film crew is like an army on the move, shifting from location to location and set to set, and needs a huge amount of logistical support. *Tomb Raider* came with a crew of 150 personnel, plus a supporting cast of up to 500 locals. Mobile production offices, artist's caravans, generators, lighting, grips and the all-important honey wagon (that's mobile toilets to you and me), all of these were needed and much more. Not forgetting the small task of feeding hungry mouths in the middle of the jungle.

This was back in 2000 and Cambodia was only an emerging destination. Hotels and vehicles were in short supply, but some adept juggling made things work. The lucky ones were housed in the Sofitel Royal Angkor, the unlucky ones had to make do with the City Angkor, soon renamed the Shitty Angkor by the construction boys. However, when it came to film servicing equipment, nothing was available, so we had to turn to Thailand.

Back in 2000, the road from Siem Reap to Poipet was notorious for potholes the size of golf bunkers and bridges that vanished into muddy brown waters. On a bad day it could take twenty-four hours to travel 150 kilometers, sometimes more. The film containers had already had a chastening experience upon arrival in Cambodia. The bridge at Stoeng, about a hundred kilometers southeast of Siem Reap, had collapsed, so the trucks had to travel the long way round via Battambang. It took them four days to arrive from Phnom Penh, a distance of 456 kilometers, and the photos were a trucker's vision of hell. Now it was the turn of the sophisticated service vehicles from Thailand, a fleet of thirty-five trucks provided by the indomitable VS Service.

First we needed a plan to deal with all the broken bridges. Two army units were contracted, travelling in six-wheel-drive Russian trucks complete with enough lumber to build bridges as the convoy rumbled along. Clearing the border was a challenge in itself, as Cambodian customs had never seen anything quite like this before. Paperwork in order, eventually the convoy moved out, one army truck pushing ahead to build a bridge before the rest of the convoy cautiously traversed. The bridge duly dismantled, the second army truck would forge ahead to build the next bridge. It was a bridge relay and the clock was ticking. The convoy took about six hours to travel 300 kilometers from Bangkok to Poipet. It took another twenty hours to travel the 150 kilometers from Poipet to Siem Reap. When they finally arrived at about four o'clock in the morning, local motorbike taxi drivers were terrified that the Thais were invading.

Finding parking spaces for thirty-five trucks was the next problem, especially in the dark. One of the artist's caravans was just that, an old tow-bar caravan that you might see in a European campsite. The big motor homes were bagged by the big stars, but even the support actors from the US often had clauses in their contracts that specified a caravan. This particular caravan had been loaded on a panel truck at Poipet and sealed for safety. When the panels were removed in Siem Reap, large sections of the caravan fell apart, like something from a Hanna-Barbera cartoon.

Angkor Wat presented a major challenge, as it is the national symbol of Cambodia and an affirmation of identity for the Cambodian people. The authorities were very concerned about filming at this national icon. To complicate matters further, President Jiang Zemin of China, on a state visit to Angkor, was due to arrive on November 14, just three days before the *Tomb Raider* shoot at the temple. He was being guided by King Sihanouk, head of state and last of the god-kings. So the authorities were adamant that the floating village could not be set up until the state visit was complete, despite King Sihanouk's well-documented obsession with film. So the floating village was built and tested on a pond in Siem Reap before being moved into Angkor Wat and dressed.

The governor of Siem Reap took rather a liking to the village and asked to spend the night there before the shoot. Even more complicated was a busload of extras arriving at Angkor Wat the night before the shoot, planning to sleep in the stilted houses.

Apsara Authority said a firm no, so we had to find beds for fifty people to spend the night. Eventually, however, the Angkor Wat shooting wrapped without incident, and it turned out to be one of the highlights of the Cambodia sequences with the incredible color and life of the floating village and the hypnotic chanting of a hundred monks.

Back to the East Gate: breaking into the 'tomb' was one of the most difficult sequences to film on the whole shoot. The giant polystyrene *apsara* needed to come tumbling down at exactly the right moment to give the appearance that it was being pulled over by the Cambodian laborers. In fact, there was a truck positioned behind the gate complete with a hydraulic arm, which would actually push the *apsara* down on cue. Rehearsals began but we had to move cautiously with four cameras set up to capture the action.

We were working with village people – no, not the seminal disco band from the '70s, but real Cambodians from around the temples with no previous exposure to film or television. The first rehearsal saw the ropes flapping around in the breeze, as the extras showed no emotion or effort. The second time they pulled harder, so hard that they almost pulled the *apsara* down. A few more practices and it was time to go live. The assistant directors barked instructions, the crowd began pulling and down came the giant *apsara* in a flurry of dust. The Cambodian extras cheered spontaneously, an unrehearsed scene that made the final cut.

Incidentally, that was the same day Angelina Jolie requested a snake. We had snake hunters on set to keep snakes away from the set. For Angelina, it was her Billy Bob Thornton period and snakes seemed to hold a peculiar fascination. Our snake hunters were duly dispatched to find a nonvenomous snake for Lara Croft and within minutes they were back. She was thrilled but the rest of the cast and crew looked decidedly worried that they had located the snake so quickly.

The tornado that was *Tomb Raider* eventually blew out of town, leaving Siem Reap with a short-term hangover. The police were sad to see it go, as they had been making money from the catering setup. This was budgeted to cater to 300 people, but on the first day, a bill arrived for 500 as the police had been selling cheap lunches to the locals. To overcome this problem of petty corruption, a raffle ticket system was introduced, but the police soon wised up to this and bought their own book of tickets.

Ultimately, these were only minor annoyances along the way. The impossible had been achieved. A major feature film had come to Cambodia and filmed the temples of Angkor. Cambodia was back on the map.

Now some of you may have been hoping for a bit more gossip on Angelina Jolie or Daniel Craig. Lara Croft and James Bond, that would have been an interesting match-up, no? Sorry, but for that sort of perspective, you need to pick up a copy of *National Enquirer* or *Hello!* But I can tell you that Angelina fell for Cambodia in a big way and adopted a young Cambodian boy named Maddox – and the rest, as they say, is history. And Daniel Craig was catapulted from relative obscurity to the Hollywood A-list.

So what are the chances of James Bond making it over to Cambodia for a little caper? Well, it's more likely we'll see Jason Bourne or Indiana Jones cavorting around Angkor than 007. But then again, life doesn't always follow the script ...

Stalking Monks in Thailand

JOE CUMMINGS

Joe Cummings was born in New Orleans and raised in California, France and Washington, DC. An interest in Buddhism drew him to Thailand, where he taught at King Mongkut's Institute of Technology Ladkrabang before returning to the US to earn a master's degree in Thai language and Southeast Asian art history at the University of California at Berkeley. He returned to Thailand to create the first Lonely Planet *Thailand* guide, which was followed by four other new titles as well as updates for other countries in the region. Other books he has written include *Buddhist Stupas in Asia; The Buddhist Temples of Thailand; Burmese Art, Design & Architecture; A Golden Souvenir of Muay Thai; Chiang Mai Style;* and *Lanna Renaissance.* His latest is *Sacred Tattoos of Thailand: Exploring the Magic, the Mastery & the Mystery of Sak Yan*. He has had small roles in several feature films. Joe also assists companies producing feature films and documentaries in Thailand, where he now resides.

Eighty-year-old director Jean-Claude Lubtchansky makes movies with esoteric, spiritual themes set in exotic lands, I was told. He wants to film a documentary on Buddhism, part of which would be shot in Thailand. Could I assist?

'He wants to create a magical set showing a large group of monks praying with a fabulous temple backdrop at magic hour,' said an email I received from a go-between. 'Also, a scene with some monks in the forest.'

Buddhism had drawn me to Thailand in the first place, and even though today I can't say that's what has kept me here, I readily accepted the job. After a few details were negotiated, Lubtchansky and producer Carlos Vejarano hired me to work on the Thailand segment, although filming would extend to sites in India, Nepal and Bhutan as well.

Planning began months before the crew's arrival in Thailand. Thomas Kelly, a veteran photographer ('photo-activist' according to his website) who first came to Nepal as a Peace Corps volunteer in 1978, served as an initial liaison between me and the crew, emailing frequently.

Two months before the crew's scheduled arrival, Thomas flew to Bangkok to discuss locations and subjects. I short-listed Buddhist monasteries I thought would work best for the production crew during their four-day shoot. Thomas meticulously photographed the locations and, after returning to his Kathmandu home, printed tidy summaries of each, matching images with prose descriptions, names of monks and monastery schedules.

Arranging a government permit to film in Thailand, along with work permit waivers for the crew, involved a hundred emails back and forth between Paris, Kathmandu and Bangkok. In Bangkok I needed a government-licensed production company to submit the forms, so I contacted Tom Waller at De Warrenne Pictures, with whom I'd worked on The Elephant King a few years earlier. Tom patiently reiterated the need for photos of the crew, passport scans, a story synopsis and an equipment list. Filling in all the gaps and finalizing the complete package, however, seemed to elude us, week after week.

In the meantime I read up on Lubtchansky. The Frenchman's career started with a bang when he edited *Lord of the Flies*, the controversial 1963 Peter Brook film adaptation of the novel of the same name. He later earned a reputation as a probing documentary director. He is particularly known for his involvement in five films dealing with the life and teachings of GI Gurdjieff, the late Greek-Armenian mystic who after a lifetime of spiritual study in Central Asia and Egypt developed the Fourth Way, a system blending metaphysics, meditation and dance.

Lubtchansky's *Georges Gurdjieff* (1976) led to a role as script consultant for Peter Brook's *Meetings with Remarkable Men* (1979), based on the mystic's autobiography. Both films so engaged the Seekers of Truth (as Gurdjieff's followers sometimes call themselves) that Lubtchansky later directed a documentary film trilogy meant to be viewed only within the circle of practitioners. I was to learn that nowadays the director was for the most part interested in making only films of this sort, documentaries to be watched by the followers of whichever tradition he explored. His documentary on Buddhism was underwritten by the Axis Mundi Foundation, I was told, and intended for Buddhist audiences.

The day the crew are set to fly to Bangkok, the film permit still hasn't been issued. Waller says not to worry, that by the time we begin shooting, we'll have it.

>>>>>>>>>>>>>>>>

When I finally greet the director in Bangkok, fresh off a flight from Paris, I feel a shock of recognition. His handlebar moustache, shaved head, deep-set eyes and tranquil disposition bring to mind photos of Gurdjieff himself.

Equally striking is Carlos Vejarano, whose tall, rail-thin frame is enlivened by a regal Spanish countenance topped with thick, silver hair. He heads the Geneva-based Axis Mundi Foundation, which is funding Lubtchansky's documentary as the second installment in a cultural-spiritual film series dubbed 'Living Prayer.' Like Lubtchansky, Vejarano projects a certain kind of calmness that suggests a lifetime of inner exploration. Later I learn he also manages the Seychelles island estate of Lillian Bettencourt, the L'Oreal heiress said to be the second richest woman in the world.

Richard Temple, owner of London's Temple Gallery and a world expert on Russian icons, completes the triumvirate of global cultural sages overseeing the film. Temple has come along at Vejarano's invitation because for many years he has visited Thailand regularly to participate in *vipassana* (Buddhist insight meditation) retreats. The highly venerated abbot of Wat Phra That Chom Thong, one of the monasteries where we will be shooting, is in fact Temple's guiding light.

Rounding out the crew are Mikael Lubtchansky, bearded son of Jean-Claude, to handle the Red videocam, and William Long, a handsome young Australian responsible for audio recording.

At our first dinner together at the Novotel Suvarnabhumi Bangkok, the director makes it clear that they do not want to film rituals or sermons.

'We want monks who are practicing the tradition and who can show us their practice by example,' he explains to me in solemn, Parisian-accented tones. 'And it has to be real.'

That night I retire to my room wondering whether I'll be able to pull this off. I have several monasteries up north ready to receive the camera team. I've explained the purpose of the documentary to the abbots and trustees, and have been assured that they can deliver monks willing to be filmed while practicing. But the crew will be shooting during the annual Magha Puja festival, which commemorates a spontaneous gathering of 1250 enlightened monks who went to hear the Buddha speak without prior summons. It's one of the most beautiful festivals of the Thai Buddhist calendar, culminating in candle-lit circumambulations of temple buildings all over Thailand.

I'm not sure this is what the director wants. And I'm not sure the film permit will arrive in time.

>>>>>>>>>>>>>>>

The following morning at check-in for our flight to Chiang Mai, a small, round-faced Thai minder sent by the film board arrives with thick, sealed envelopes containing our film permit and work permit waivers. He will accompany us for the entire shoot, as mandated by Thai law.

Much relieved that we are now a legal foreign film production crew, we fly to Chiang Mai, where I've arranged for two vans to transport the team and camera gear to our first location. In Mae Rim, a semirural district north of Chiang Mai, Dhamma Drops is a modern retreat center affiliated with Sulak

Sivaraksa, the nation's most well-known Buddhist social activist. We receive a warm welcome from Phra Ta, the monk in charge of the center, which has been open only a year and is still partially under construction.

Phra Ta has arranged for the crew to film around twenty monks mediating in three locations: a teak forest, a mango grove and a large teak-pillared pavilion overlooking the Mae Raem river. In the teak forest the monks hang cone-shaped mosquito nets from the trees and sit cross-legged beneath them, hardly moving a limb for an hour. They then pile into the vans and visit the other two locations for more sitting meditation, but without nets, since the mango grove is quite shady and the pavilion roofed.

The filming goes well, and the shot reviews look amazing. Lubchantsky praises the shoot but I can sense from his silence during lunch that having such activities contrived for our benefit falls short of his objectives.

After thanking the monks for their kind assistance, and leaving them with a sizable cash donation, we proceed to our next stop, Wat Umong.

Founded in the fifteenth century when Chiang Mai flourished as the capital of the Lanna Kingdom, Wat Umong (Tunnel Monastery) lay semi-abandoned after Burmese invasions 300 years later. Buddhadasa Bhikkhu, the most famous Thai monk of the late twentieth century, revived the wat in the 1970s to serve as a northern branch of his well-known home monastery in the south, Wat Suan Mokkhaphalaram. Today it is considered one of the more serious monastic centers in Chiang Mai.

Here the abbot graciously lends us about a dozen monks, and as I arranged earlier in the week, they practice walking meditation around a large stupa surmounting a flat-topped hill on the grounds. The afternoon light is sublime, and the crew captures atmospheric footage of the ochre-robed men silently circumambulating the ancient monument.

I then lead the crew and a smaller contingent of six monks to the monastery's namesake tunnels, dug into the hillside centuries ago and lined with brick to serve as a cool meditation refuge. At one time the tunnels were reserved for monks and Lanna royalty only, but nowadays they are open to the public. Empty niches in the walls once held myriad votive Buddha statues, and in a few spots faint traces of mural paintings can still be made out.

Here the crew shoots the monks sitting in meditation in one of the smaller side tunnels, then walking single-file through one of the larger ones. Lit only by the last rays of the day's sun feeding horizontally through the end of the tunnel, the scene seems tailor-made for documentary cinema, I feel.

From Chiang Mai we head southwest into the night to reach the small town of Chom Thong, where we make our way to the Northern Thailand Insight Meditation Center behind Wat Phra That Si Chom Thong. The sprawling collection of white-painted, one-story houses resembles a suburban subdivision, and is run by a Thai-American couple, Thanat and Kathryn Chindaporn. They graciously accommodate the entire crew in one of the meditation bungalows.

A huge, near-full moon looms over the monastery, and tomorrow on the full moon day itself, a majestic series of ceremonies will take place. Hundreds of monks from around the north will assemble in the courtyard surrounding the main chapel, to chant mantras in unison while a gilded pinnacle is installed over the massive carved wooden doors.

It's a scene most filmmakers would leap for joy to record, but when I describe the planned proceedings, Lubtchansky makes it clear he isn't interested in the slightest. For him, Buddhist practice is meditation, not chanting.

Kathryn has suggested taking the crew to Wat Tham Thong, a forest hermitage about an hour's drive east, the following day. There we are sure to find monks in meditation, even on a major Buddhist holiday like this. Lubtchansky and the crew agree, and I retire to a thin mattress on the floor hoping that the next day will bring us what we need to wrap up the filming. There is only one full day left in our schedule.

>>>>>>>>>>>>>>>>

We awake to the sound of chanting monks, then share a silent meal of tea and rice porridge before attending a private 7am audience with Ajahn Tong Sirimangalo, abbot of Wat Phra That Si Chom Thong.

Even though Thomas Kelly has told me Lubtchansky didn't want to listen to monks expounding Buddhism, I have convinced the director that it would be rude not to take the opportunity to see the abbot since we were guests of his monastery.

The abbot's assistants lead us to a large, sunny hall with a raised dais and altar at one end, where we are to wait for Ajahn Tong. As a young monk he had studied *satipatthana* (mindfulness) meditation in Myanamr for two years, and was one of the first Thai monks to introduce the system in Thailand. At eighty-nine years old, he is not only the highest-ranking monk in northern Thailand, he is also one of the foremost living masters of meditation in the country. For me it feels like a rare honor and privilege for the seven of us to be introduced to him.

Ajahn Tong arrives unannounced and without even glancing our way, slowly hoists his heavy body up the short flight of steps onto the dais. His shaven head is mottled with age spots, and his glasses sit crookedly on his nose. After prostrating three times before the gilded Buddha image on the altar, the abbot sits cross-legged and begins chanting in a low, steady voice. Meanwhile the Red camera is rolling.

His prayers finished, the elderly monk turns around to face us, still cross-legged. Kathryn translates as Lubtchansky and Temple ask questions about the spiritual life. Ajahn Tong's answers are brief and carry a sense of urgency, as if he wants to impress upon us that every moment spent on worldly affairs – such as making this film – is a waste of time.

'Everything you need to learn about Buddhism is right here within the confines of this body, and this mind,' he says at one point. 'No need to go anywhere or read anything. Study what you are born with. What you are seeking is here, nowhere else.'

And then the audience is over, and our vans are negotiating mountain curves en route to our final location, Wat Tham Thong. We arrive just in time to observe the resident monks standing in a long, neat row at the base of a limestone cliff, cradling black alms bowls in their hands to receive alms food from the laity on this auspicious full-moon day.

It's more ritual, and while one camera dutifully captures it all, I take Lubtchansky for a stroll alongside a stream at the back of the forest monastery to show him a series of limestone caves in the cliffs. Most of the caves have small Buddha altars where laypeople leave offerings of candles, incense and flowers.

We hoped to find monks meditating in the caves, but they're empty. Luckily abbot Ajahn Sujin Vimalo, a wizened little man with large ears, lends us a few resident monks who accompany us to an isolated cave set high in a limestone cliff, reached by a steep set of cement stairs. Sitting in a semi-circle on the cave floor, they do a bit of chanting before settling into a session of sitting meditation.

The cameras shift from angle to angle in the cave, but the row of shaved, silent heads isn't so different from the group shots in the teak forest the day before. Virtually all of our shots so far have been set-ups, in fact, high on visuals and atmosphere but I'm not sure the director is getting what he really wants. His words come back to me: 'And it has to be real.'

Bored with the cave scene and knowing the crew will be shooting for another half hour or more, I leave for a walk. Rather than head back to the main monastery buildings, I follow a leaf-strewn path above and parallel to the Mae Jaem river as it zigzags through monsoon forest and along the sheer cliffs, flowing towards deep, narrow Ob Luang Gorge.

The path quickly becomes steep and rocky. I could turn back but I feel something drawing me on, some force quickening my step. The path narrows, then fades out entirely at an incline, where I try to stop myself but, slipping on tropical dew coating a thick layer of leaves, I go down on my ass, the thrumming sound of the stream growing louder as I slide nearly all the way to the water's edge.

I struggle to my feet, brushing away dirt and forest debris from my clothes, and find myself staring at an otherworldly tableau of crystalline waters and smooth-topped boulders. One large stone splits the river in two, creating a calm eddy in its lee. I make out a whirlpool at the centre of the eddy, and above the whirlpool, a flash of ochre.

A thick blanket is slung around the shoulders of his outer robe, and above that, his head gleams in the fading daylight. The dusky hue of his robes suggests that he dyed them himself, probably using jackfruit heartwood. His skin, burned walnut from exposure to sun and wind, suggests he's a *tudong* monk who takes on extra ascetic practices, including a vow not to dwell under a roof.

Considering the racket I made sliding down the hill, I expect the monk to get up from his lotus position atop the boulder and disappear into the forest. But he doesn't move a muscle.

I rush back to the cave using a flat, dry-season path hugging the river, and tell the director about the monk in the middle of the river. Within ten minutes he has camera and sound in position, and for the next hour, until the sun dips below the treetops, the team films the lone forest monk from every possible angle.

The monk never shifts from his position the entire time, never opens his eyes, never gives any indication that he knows we're there.

'That was the money shot,' the director's son Mikael tells me over dinner that evening back in Chom Thong.

Sunrise in Balibo

ROBERT CONNOLLY

Robert Connolly travelled to East Timor in 2008 to make the feature film *Balibo*. It premiered at the Melbourne, Toronto, Sao Paulo and London film festivals. His previous directing credits include the award-winning political feature films *The Bank* and *Three Dollars*. In 2009 he was awarded the Timorese Presidential Medal of Merit as part of the nation's ten-year anniversary of independence celebrations, in recognition of the role the film *Balibo* had in telling an important part of the nation's history for the first time on film.

In 2009 I took a small film crew to East Timor to make the feature film *Balibo,* a story depicting the events surrounding the Indonesian invasion of this newly independent nation in 1975.

Twelve months earlier I had headed to East Timor to meet and attempt to convince Nobel Laureate and President José Ramos-Horta that making the film in his country, in the places where the tragic events in the film had actually happened, was worth supporting.

This trip and meeting were made more complex because the screenplay depicted Ramos-Horta as the much younger man he was in 1975, an infamous Che Guevara–like revolutionary, consummate womanizer and formidable diplomat.

Refusing to live in a more formal presidential palace, Ramos-Horta's home is a far more humble traditional structure, just east of the heart of the nation's capital, Dili, and a five-minute walk to the beach. Six months later, a failed attack would see him take three bullets in the gut in the very home we arrived at to argue our case.

I had sent the screenplay ahead, uncensored (despite my better judgment that softening the edges might have made our task easier), together with a DVD starring the actor we proposed to play his younger self.

'This actor,' he began immediately after we arrived, 'I have shown his film to some close friends, women. "Is he good looking enough to play me?" I asked them. "No", they all agreed. "Certainly not." George Clooney I was thinking would be better, what do you think?' A cheeky, playful twinkle in his eye betrayed his mischief.

He was curious about our first impressions of East Timor. The impact of Indonesia's savage withdrawal in 1999 was everywhere: sprawling displaced-persons' camps surrounded the airport, United Nations and Australian troops patrolled the streets, almost the entire infrastructure remained damaged in some way. At the airport in Darwin that very day, we told him, the Australian government had raised the security advice for travel to East Timor to only one step beneath post-invasion Baghdad.

The travel warnings clearly frustrated him; they discouraged tourism and investment. The US warnings were the same, he said. East Timor was, as we found while filming, as safe as Ramos-Horta had promised us that night over dinner. In one minor public joke to make a point he had posted an official warning to East Timorese travelling to New York: 'Please be advised that if you are dark of skin, using the subway in certain parts of New York is unsafe.'

The shoot would require permission to film in the remote town of Balibo, where five young journalists had been murdered by invading Indonesian troops to conceal the truth of a covert military incursion. Ramos-Horta had been in Balibo in 1975 with the journalists and had warned them of the dangers before heading back to Dili to await the full-scale Indonesian invasion that would happen by sea and air only a few months later. The world would turn a blind eye.

Ironically, in the heart of Balibo, a statue looks down on the town square where the journalists were killed. A relic from the Indonesian occupation, it depicts a man breaking chains, the shackles of colonial occupation. After 400 years of Portuguese rule, the Timorese enjoyed only nine days of independence before Indonesia claimed this small nation as its own. Ramos-Horta offered that night to tear it down if it would make filming easier, and gave us the permission we needed to move ahead.

Four hours' drive from Dili, Balibo sits on a strategically high vantage point looking down towards the Ombai Strait and the border with Indonesian West Timor. A 400-year-old fort built by the Portuguese continues to take military advantage of this extraordinary location, with Australian troops stationed there in 1999.

On the evening before we recreated the Indonesian invasion of Balibo and murder of the journalists, Lieutenant Colonel Sabika turned up with Ramos-Horta's blessing, together with over a hundred of his troops. Not only would they help depict the invasion by playing the invading soldiers, Sabika himself would be our guide. As a young commander in the East Timor army in 1975, he had defended Balibo on the morning of the invasion. His troops camped the night in the fort.

Looking down towards the sea at dusk, Sabika showed us where the boats had been positioned, where the troops had landed and the direction they had attacked from. It was humbling to stand there with a man who thirty-five years before had attempted to defend this town.

We slept that night next to a small church beneath the fort; the five actors chose to stay in the house the journalists had slept in the night before they died. On the wall at the front of that building, recovered beneath layers of paint, a picture of the Australian flag has been framed. The journalists had hoped it would afford them some protection.

Together, before morning, we all headed up to the fort to prepare to film.

Never before had the idea of sunrise held such significance on set. A coronial inquest had explored the reasons the journalists had remained after Sabika and his men had retreated on that fateful day. The journalists' 16-millimeter cameras required enough light to get a reasonable exposure to capture the footage of the invasion. They had perhaps stayed until the sun had only just broken the horizon in order to film – but by then it was too late, and they were murdered shortly after.

Cameras ready, we too waited for that moment, a soft light only just revealing the landscape. Amongst the many moments in filmmaking that are repetitive and dull, the more sublime moments, rare as they are, can be extraordinary. That morning remains the most moving of my career.

Standing by on that hill with the Australian and Timorese cast and crew poised to film, Sabika's troops waiting down below to recreate the attack, the anticipation was overwhelming.

The sun broke the horizon, and we began to film.

The Broome Circuit

AARON PEDERSEN

Aaron Pedersen is an Arrernte/Arabana man from Alice Springs. Whilst growing up, Aaron believed many images of Indigenous Australians on television were negatively stereotypical. After initially training as a journalist at the Australian Broadcasting Commission in Melbourne, Aaron transitioned into acting. Through his work on *Wildside*, *Water Rats*, *MDA*, *Territorians*, *Grass Roots*, *Queen of Hearts*, *BlackJack* and *The Secret Life of Us*, Aaron has been able to champion the changing representation of Indigenous people in Australia. In 2007, he won a Deadly Award for Male Actor of the Year. Most recently, Aaron was the co-lead in the Seven Network police drama, *City Homicide*, and was the lead in series one and two of the SBS miniseries, *The Circuit*, set in the Kimberley region of Western Australia.

It was late 2008 and we were nearing the end of a long and arduous three-month shoot in the Western Australian Kimberleys. We had been filming the second series of *The Circuit* in and around a very hot and humid Broome. From the very first 'turn over' the shoot felt heavier and somewhat harder.

During the shoot Broome slowly became blanketed by humidity. The buildup was so intense at times it was like working in a sauna. The weight just fell off cast and crew. Some dropped fifteen to twenty kilos. There was very little relief.

The buildup was a bonus in some way because it added extra weight to the minefield of emotionally charged moments that were woven into the stories. It brought rawness to the characters' journeys and life to the world of *The Circuit*. Its very presence became a character in the show. Every day it was there.

It was the second-to-last day and it was sweltering. We were located about fifty kilometers out of Broome filming amongst the stillness of an isolated roadhouse. It was unbearably hot especially under the lights. Some days it felt like I was being baked. This was definitely one of those days.

It was late in the afternoon and most of the cast and crew from the main unit had wrapped. For them the tireless journey was finally over. Like a shot they were back in Broome, hungering to get back to the cool ocean breeze that was to bring them relief. No doubt they were happy that their day was done. I reckoned they were down the beach soaking their sweat-drenched souls in the soothing salt water. I would have been. The crew set the bar very high. In my eyes they were best on ground.

The sun hadn't quite set on this story for me and several of the others just yet. We had one more call sheet to complete. Some might say that we were the unlucky ones, that we drew the short straw. I didn't think so. I was there at the beginning and I was keen to be there at the end. I had a good feeling about the last day's shoot.

The small convoy of cast and crew hit the road and headed further away from the luxurious coastline of Broome. We were heading to a community that was inland some three hours. Some might say that the community was in the middle of nowhere. But it wasn't, it was where it should be.

Along the way we knocked off some driving scenes for my character, Drew Ellis. There were several important moments we still had to get in the can. Some were lighthearted but the rest were soul-searching. As I was actor and director, the last day was going to be the hardest shoot day of all.

One in particular was a pickup scene for the first episode about deaths in custody. The character of Clarrie (LeRoy Parsons) was found hanging in his prison cell. Drew had lost a good mate. How was he to deal with it? There were tears. This was to set the scene for what was to come.

It was our final night together and we were camping out. Cast and crew were spending the night sleeping under the stars. We all bedded down for the night, some wrapped in their swags, some in the dirt, and some on makeshift beds on top of the four-wheel drives. It was the right way to say goodbye to the country and each other. It was good for the soul.

The last day arrived and the early morning sun was already making a statement. You could feel the temperature building up. The air was hotter out here. It made breathing hard work. Little were we to know that it was going to be the hottest and most punishing day of all, reaching a staggering sixty-seven degrees Celsius in the sun.

Everybody knew that, as an actor, I was going to take my character Drew to some emotional places that day. Drew was heading back to his homeland with the old people. Leading the way would be the man who had found him, Jack Stallion (Phillip Green), followed by his uncle Lionel (Jimmy Edgar) and his father's youngest brother, Mick (Tony Briggs). He was going to walk on his country for the first time with the men in his family. What was this going to do to him?

The one thing that I didn't get to do during the course of the shoot was a 'location recce.' I hadn't seen 'the homelands.' I was flying blind, just like Drew. We were both going to see it for the first time. Maybe that was a good thing. I wasn't sure what we were in for. Anything could happen.

It was a different part of the Kimberley. The land's character changed dramatically. This country was proud and silent. There were no pristine beaches out here, nothing close to it. The landscape felt very familiar to me, strong mountainous red cliffs like the kind that I had grown up with in Alice Springs. The only difference was the hundreds of majestic boab trees. They stood tall like guardians on the land. Maybe they were there guarding us. Guarding me.

We reached a small waterhole hidden amongst the cliffs. It was to be the place where Drew would find himself. What was this going to look like? What were we going to see? Nobody knew. Not even me.

My last piece of direction before the scene started was to ask old Jack Stallion to call to country. I needed to hear from the elders. This was to be my trigger. The scene was in motion. The land filled with silent pride. There was no stopping it now.

It all went quiet. Old Jack Stallion called once. 'Coooeee!!!!' His ancient voiced echoed off the jagged cliffs and pierced all who were present. It got me right inside me. I could feel my own heart beat. I could hear myself breathing. It was like I was outside myself. It was happening. Drew was connecting with his homeland.

The old man followed up again with four or five more sharp calls. Each time it was louder. 'Cooeeee!!!!' Shivers snaked up my spine. I literally felt the country rise up from inside me, something broke. Uncontrollably I started to shake and cry. I knew I wasn't the only one feeling it. The crew were feeling it too. We were all connecting with something, somewhere. The old men watched on. They'd been waiting for this moment. The country had found Drew.

India: A Family Portrait

STEPHANIE MARCH

Stephanie March is an actress, activist and dedicated traveler. She is best known for her role as Assistant Deputy Attorney Alexandra Cabot on *Law & Order: Special Victims Unit*. Other television appearances include *Grey's Anatomy* and *30 Rock*. She has also appeared in the films *The Treatment*, *Mr & Mrs Smith*, *The Invention of Lying* and *Head of State*, as well as several Broadway and off-Broadway productions. She is a contributing editor of Fathom at www.fathomaway.com, and a graduate of Northwestern University. Stephanie resides in New York City – when she is not plotting her next getaway.

India: A Family Portrait

Three years ago I went on a family vacation. Three fun-loving, cocktail-slugging blondes from Texas indulging in a girls' trip – my mother, sister Charlotte and me. We wanted to shop, have tea, take in a show and make fun of other relatives. We decided to do this in India.

Group travel evolves into the same basic hierarchy no matter the participants or the destination. One of the players is always In Charge. This person chooses the destination and accommodations and maps a basic itinerary of each day's events. The second person is First Mate. This person brings along guidebooks and sunscreen, suggests interesting dinners or sightseeing adventures, and is helpful to In Charge in realizing her perfect vision of the trip. First Mate's secret powers lie in her ability to shape the trip to her liking without ever engaging in direct confrontation with In Charge. Grumbler is the individual who complains in a passive aggressive fashion throughout the trip without ever actually making an effort to improve things. Grumbler wants vegetarian options. Grumbler is hot/knew we should have turned left/makes a big deal about brushing her teeth with bottled water. This dynamic has even greater meaning when the travelers in question are intimately related and have thirty years of familial power structure embedded in their DNA. Taking a family trip is sort of like this: imagine you are asked to sew a quilt for a king-sized bed. Now imagine the quilt has to be made completely of Saran Wrap. Good luck.

We reconnoitered with an overnight stutter step in Delhi (Charlotte had been in India for three weeks on her own). We took twelve hours to wash the hair, down a few gin and tonics (our preferred antimalarial), and repack the bags for our journey to Udaipur the next morning. Upon arrival at the jazzy, Western airport hotel, I discovered that my beloved film camera had died a mysterious death. No new battery, no new film, no tender wiping of gears and lenses could bring it back to life. Refusing to resign it to the ignoble grave of the hotel's garbage can, I toted it through the rest of the trip wrapped in my nightgown. And I commandeered my mother's camera, using the unassailable logic that I took much better pictures than she did (years of Christmas cards bore me out on this). Then I got busy documenting the hell out of our Indian adventure. At that moment I was In Charge. I knew exactly how to conduct this portion of the trip. I was in the arts, for heaven's sake. My whole livelihood was picture and story. I knew what I was doing – so just take your smiley, out-of-focus, stupid shot of the bougainvillea and Charlotte and me and step aside, all right?

In Udaipur I forced us into all manner of *Jewel in the Crown*–inspired tableaux. Mom and Char with a distant palace and dusky sunset behind them. Mom and Char on a cheery, leaky boat puttering out to a hotel smack in the middle of a lake. Mom and Char gazing behind marble purdah screens carved like lace. Mom insisted on taking the camera for a shot of Charlotte and me on camels and I immediately groaned about how badly she was going to frame the shot. The minute I got down (way down – God, they are tall) I scanned through her shots. I was right. They were evidence without being story and I was annoyed at her inability to capture the moment. I rolled my eyes and wordlessly showed the shots to Charlotte, who agreed with equal annoyance about how average our mother's pictures were. We were hostages no longer to her timetable, her mandatory afternoon nap, and her insistence that liver and onions were a perfectly good dinner. No sir. We were In Charge and First Mate. Hop on board or be left behind.

We carried on in this bratty fashion for the rest of the trip. We were unstoppable. Surging through me was the absolute need to assert myself. My psyche was trapped in 1989 and every instinct was one eye-rolling, smart-alecky, defiant, pathetic declaration, 'You are not the boss of me.' Charlotte and I were right, just right about all of it. Which way the cab should turn, what time the museum closes, whether or not dhal is always green lentils, and the fact that the tourist with the funny accent was South African, not British for chrissake.

It wasn't all bad. Not at all. In fact, it was magnificent. India is remarkable, even on a bad day, and there was plenty to keep us lively. In Udaipur we visited the City Palace and were squired about by Ashook, the subcontinent's most charming guide. Ashook never met a carved niche or painted miniature that did not elicit a delighted chirp. He breathlessly extolled the virtues of every portraiture artist since the days of the Mughals (about 75,000, by my count). We lunched under banyan trees and ate our weight in *paratha*. We shared suppressed giggles every time someone mentioned the movie *Octopussy* – filmed at our hotel and handily the most popular local fact. Honestly, you could spend a week in Udaipur and not hear a word about Kipling. Try to go ten minutes without having a copy of *Octopussy* forced into your hand and it's another matter entirely. One night we finally succumbed and piled into Mom's room with a bottle of Scotch and the DVD. It was like getting a good kiss from someone you don't like – impossible to ignore and leaving a weird queasiness.

In Kerala, I corralled the girls into smiley scenes on the slim wooden boat that silently bore us through tiger-eyed backwaters. The man steering the boat was the color of coal and had hands like rocks. We discovered cardamom coffee at our hotel (a treat I continue in New York City) and drank coconut water at every breakfast. Across the hotel there was a cheerily lit, thatched-roof theater housing a Kathakali dance company and several touring musicians. We attended performances and marveled, along with a dozen feral cats running across the rafters, at the heart-stopping talents of both. I will never forget the dancer who moved forty-seven different muscles in his face, one at a time, to the beat of a drum. I captured all of it with an energy boarding on mania using my mom's digital camera. Having been liberated from the tyranny of film rationing, I began to construct a monster masterpiece of our Perfectly Documented Trip.

We careened from one magical, uncomfortable, sweat-stained adventure to the next, bickering and giggling and nagging. Nagging my poor mother about her luggage, which was distinctly not of the carry-on variety. Rolling our eyes over her hot rollers and her need to plug her ears when she flew and the way she flagged the túk-túks. We sighed over her terrified shrieks in Mumbai's asteroid traffic. We were funny, clever little shits who could not stop ourselves from reverting into past behavior. What was it? What was this thing that made us all one heart and three loud mouths? What was this unexpected, unaccountable need to prove who was in charge?

By the time we got to Agra we had added twenty pounds of luggage consisting mostly of textiles, earrings and a crazy delicious curried snack mix from a spice market in Mumbai. Fun culinary gifts for home! We had consumed a shocking quantity of Bombay gin to smooth our rough edges. For the final act in our epic we decided to dress in saris and get a group shot in front of the Taj Mahal. If it makes you groan to read that, consider this: very often the best way to surmount the inevitable cliché of a moment is to wholly embrace the cliché. We didn't have a snowball's chance in hell of having a truly artful photo taken of the three of us. I mean, who but me could really accomplish that and I was going to have to be in the picture, right? Embrace the obvious. Gleefully busk for a moment. My plan was to arrange Charlotte and Mom in position with the Taj behind them, step in myself, and coerce a German tourist into taking a few snaps. I decided on a German because everyone knows they can work expensive machinery and they take a very no-nonsense approach to fun. We needed a precision individual who could follow direction.

We were grouchy because it was early, we'd been traveling for two weeks, and tea, oddly, did not come in twenty-ounce to-go containers in India. When you go to a tea shop, you have to sit and drink your drink. On the grounds of the Taj we were overwhelmed by hustlers. They would not stop badgering us. They were kudzu. Everywhere we turned one was at our side, at our feet, and on our back chat-chat-chattering for us to 'Buy this, lady.' Postcards, figurines, incense, jewelry, playing cards, shot glasses, even guys taking twenty-dollar digital photographs. A less fatigued version of me would have been more sympathetic – my God, I know it's hard to make a living in some places. But I was not that person that day. I was the focused, brusque traveler on a mission and nothing was going to stop me from completing my masterpiece. This photo essay, no photo sympathy, of our trip demanded a terrific shot of the Taj. My dress was all sari, my attitude all clipboard and headset.

It should be noted that the Taj Mahal is even more splendid in real life. It looks like the movie of itself. It is creamy and swooping and all poem and anthem. There are not enough superlatives to describe its mathematical precision. It is a masterpiece of love and suffering and it must be captured with majesty. Obviously this was a job for me. I busily arranged the girls into perfect composition. It wasn't easy trying to maximize views of the building and minimize the wandering herds of packish Japanese tourists but I did it. We flagged someone to take the photo (I honestly cannot recall her nationality) and checked it off our list of life's things to do. Then in a moment of confusion my mother okayed a shot from one of the Agra hustlers and Charlotte and I were utterly contemptuous. Twenty dollars for a digital photograph? We've got it worked out. For heaven's sake. Just be quiet and let us deal with this. She quietly paid him for his troubles and pocketed a decent, if not completely in-focus, picture. Whatever.

Four days later we landed at Newark, groggy and rotten from the long flight. I had spent three hours on the plane editing and cutting and perfecting the album. If you like taking pictures, you damn well better go to India. You cannot miss. Spice markets, temples, painted elephants, monkeys on rooftops, dusty pink sunsets, jungles – I had it all. Well, I thought I did.

It was in the car on the way home that I realized with a sickening, stomach-dropping thud that the camera was gone. Gone. Vanished. Utterly not there. No amount of frantic tearing apart of luggage could coax it from the ether. I was completely beside myself. It must have slid out of my purse and disappeared in the rows behind me. Or it was stolen. Or it was buried under newspapers, plastic wrappers, tissues and all the other detritus of a sixteen-hour flight. Or the gods were angry.

The entire catalogue of moments was wiped from existence. Every last image, from the neon-lit bar in Delhi, to the dancing boys in saffron turbans, to the cow draped in conch shells, to my mother's coquettish smile at the Red Fort and Charlotte's profile against the Arabian Sea – it was lost forever. Even as I write this, three years later, I feel vaguely nauseous.

When I told my sister and mother, they were startlingly and touchingly reassuring. 'It's not your fault. These things happen. It's the memories that count, not pictures ...' For three weeks I had insisted I was the only one of us who could adequately capture our trip. A barking Kodak Napoleon whose vision could only be achieved through total command. All proof of my newfound authority and rigorous control of the adventure had vanished. Stupid. Silly. Shameful. It was with a familiar contrition and slinking shame that I called my mother to apologize. We did not have one goddamn picture of our entire adventure.

Well, not quite. There was one photo. One grainy, out-of-focus photo of three blonde ladies, dolled up in a rainbow of saris and wrapped in shawls grinning against early-morning chill. The Taj Mahal arcs behind them. It took ten seconds to take and cost twenty dollars.

I have my mother to thank for that.

The Call of Morocco

SANDRA BERNHARD

Sandra Bernhard is an actress and a performer. She has authored three books and her writing has also appeared in numerous publications, among them the *New Yorker*, *Vanity Fair* and *Condé Nast Traveler*. She lives in New York City with her girlfriend and daughter.

What led me to Morocco on three different occasions was a sense of desperation. To go back to a place I had dreamed of, imagined and longed for. Nothing came close to the emotion and desire I felt staring at the map of North Africa. It called to me as if I'd been there in a hundred other lifetimes.

On my second journey to Morocco, things were quite different. In the years since my first carefree, spontaneous trip, I had become a mother. Though still a gypsy at heart (with a strong desire for beautiful sheets and a top-of-the-line mattress), some focus on detail had become paramount. Obsessed with all things organic, I started to panic; what would I feed Cicely (my child) once we arrived in this land without amenities? I checked in with my friend Soumaya, who would be hosting us in her family home in the Kasbah of Tangier.

Soumaya seemed nonplussed by the whole conversation and simply gave me her address. I sent out the troops to gather cases of organic baby food, formula, diapers – you would have thought we were headed into some sort of gulag. We packed all this up in big boxes, carefully wrapping each bottle, then alerted UPS and in they came to haul them away. I ran after them, saying, 'Please be careful. That is precious cargo. It must arrive at its destination safely!'

Then I sat for a while thinking about its journey and my own. This was a huge trip. I was bringing the whole gang: Cicely, her nanny Vicky, who at age ten had found her way up from Guatemala, alone, to rejoin her mother Anita in LA (Anita had left to find work in America a few years earlier so that she could support her children back home, even though she knew she might never see them again), Mitch, my musical director, and Breanne, my assistant from Garretson Beach, Brooklyn. We all headed out to JFK airport and boarded our flight to Tangier via London, an American Airlines extravaganza, with an endowment from various gigs and writing assignments that would be folded into this major excursion.

I insisted on wearing my white straw cowboy hat on the trip and it became a kind of annoying mascot along the way. I left it in the overhead bin on the London flight, and this occasioned a major catastrophe as I ran around tracking down special services to bring it to me in baggage claim. This was an ugly way to start our travels, but I couldn't move forward without that hat. As Breanne would often say in her thick Brooklynese accent throughout the trip, 'If you're looking for Sandra, she's the one with steam rising out of the top of her cowboy hat.'

After a refreshing night at the Heathrow Hilton, we regrouped and headed off to our destination. Glitches continued. At Moroccan customs we discovered that Vicky did need a visa 'after all.' Soumaya and her father, Absalim, who had taken over by this point, remained calm –after all, this is a man who lives by the credo 'America may have the clock, but we have the time.' My patience, not one of my stronger virtues anyway, was worn paper-thin by this point. But Daddy told us all to go on to the house, he'd stay behind to sort things out. I wept throughout the car ride, wondering what I would do without my stalwart (albeit sometimes crazy stalwart) Vicky G.

We arrived at the edge of the Kasbah to much excitement and glamour; the cars stopped and out ran a cadre of jalaba-festooned gentlemen with carts to carry away our baggage. The family in the main house welcomed us all for an immediate glass of Moroccan whisky (mint tea) and we sat in the entry courtyard as the sun came down. Twinkling candles were lit all around, and Soumaya introduced us to the household. Of course, there was Mama, Khadush, who was incredibly chic and a mother to all. She held Cicely and fussed over her. I nervously asked, 'Has the baby's food arrived?' That brought the house down. Sideways glances between all the ladies led me to believe that this had been looked on as a folly. Khadush hugged me, saying, 'We will make the baby fresh foods; she does not want this stuff that has traveled longer than you!'

Off she swept the baby, to the heart of the house, the kitchen, where the main cook, Khadisha, tucked Cicely into a strong cloth that she tied over her shoulder. Cicely's little head popped out of the top, delighted. The baby was totally relaxed as Khadisha went about her chores, sweeping up, stirring the pots of couscous on the stove, checking on the tagines already fired up for our dinner. When she checked the pita bread baking in the ovens, bending over to see, I held my breath, afraid Cicely might slide out onto the floor. But all was well.

Khadisha continued moving about as I noticed, there in the corner, the box I had shipped six weeks earlier. It was battered and wrecked, torn open in one corner; I sheepishly went over and peered inside. The contents were intact but seemed somehow pathetic in this setting of all things fresh: eggs sitting out on the tiled counter, ceramic bowls filled with tangerines and aubergines, courgettes and figs, cilantro, tomatoes, and the aromatic spices that are dried and customized in each household into a blend called *ras al hanout*, which translates as 'the head of the house' – pungent, intoxicating, seductive. Against this plentiful backdrop sat my sad wares, which I had spent hours buying, wrapping and packing – not to mention the $600 for shipping. The box remained in its place in the corner during our entire stay. I never looked at it again.

Word of Vicky came in the late hours before we slept: she would be returned to us the next day after some official pardon had been approved. Exhausted and raw, I fell asleep and woke early in the morning to the first sounds of the *muezzin* calling the righteous to prayer. From the minarets the calls came, like sirens rising in the distance; they grew closer and I was startled at first, but then I laid back down and the voices soothed me. After two days, I couldn't even hear them anymore.

One of the highlights of our stay in Tangier was the amazing cuisine, thanks to the endless talents of Soumaya, her mother, and all the ladies who arrived at the crack of dawn and stayed until long after sundown. We ate porridge for breakfast, fresh fish or *bastilla* for lunch, mint tea and honey-laden cookies at four o'clock.

Dinner was a feast: vegetables over couscous, lamb and prune tagine, spicy meatballs in a tomato sauce, everything cooking right up until it was eaten, sometimes in the kitchen, other times in the courtyard, where the world was shut out behind heavy wooden doors and friends came in to have crazy high-spirited conversations splashed with French and English.

Tangier is filled with expatriates, from America, Great Britain, France. One day we stopped by to visit the ex-head of a Colombian cartel, who had fled and was now living on the down low and enjoying the privacy and sophistication of Morocco, his past barely acknowledged and simply brushed away.

Absalim knew everyone in town. We tagged along to sit with him and pay visits to those he had grown close to. Paul Bowles welcomed us into his small abode; on his side table were a stack of *High Times*. I shook his frail hand, 'I am so happy to meet you.'

He was sitting on the edge of his twin bed with Mickey Mouse sheets. He replied, 'I'm so happy that I'm able to make you happy, my dear.'

We hung out for a while chatting about the day and the changes that were coming. It seemed as if this was an old routine for him; well-wishers and nosy intruders were part of his daily ritual.

One early evening Mitch, Breanne and I wandered right outside the Kasbah to a small smoky café where music was just getting started; violins, *qsbah* (flutes), *ghita* (a skinny guitar), *ta'arija* (drums) and more instruments joined in the classic melodies of *Chaabi* fused with jazz and other international influences. The men looked at us with some suspicious humor, nodding, lost in their groove, the songs stirring up and down, building to momentous peaks and falling almost hushed until you could feel the breathing in the room. The musicians asked if we would like to continue the jam session in someone's home where we could also enjoy some hashish.

We left a generous tip and attempted to thank them all in many broken languages: *'Merci,' 'Shukran,' 'Inshallah.'* (I've been using those last two words ever since, whenever possible, really, bandying them about as if whole conversations might be at the tip of my tongue.) After that, we wandered into the dusk where we stopped to look out at the views of the Mediterranean, the Straits of Gibraltar, and the southern tip of Spain, disappearing into darkness. Then we headed back for dinner.

>>>>>>>>>>>>>>>

The drama of Fès rose in front of us as we flew in and seemingly back in time, where everything looked as it must have 5000 years before. The sun beat down on the ancient souq as we landed and headed to the classic beauty of the hotel Palais Jamais located at the mouth of the *medina*. We settled into our rooms, Cicely wide-eyed, being swept around like the tiniest tourist, rolling with the punches of it all, the perfect traveler. We headed down to the bar and sipped gin and tonics and picked at the nuts, steadying ourselves for what we had been assured would be the craziest experience of our travels.

A young boy loitering outside the hotel offered his services as a guide. We bartered back and forth and almost walked off before he relented and accepted (what we thought was) our very generous offer. Off we went, leaving the little one behind with Vicky, who happily relaxed poolside with a club sandwich, fries and a Coke.

Into the heart and soul of Fès we went, our guide leading us left and suddenly right, winding up stairs, struggling between donkeys laden with baskets of bricks, goats ninnying and butting heads, stall after stall of every kind of olive known to mankind, Berber ladies with red-stained teeth and men wearing the hats of their hometowns. At one point I came upon rows of leather goods where I spotted my beloved 'satchel,' a handmade leather bag just big enough for credit cards, some cash and one set of keys. I still carry it to this day (in spite of its wretched condition), much to the chagrin of my girlfriend Sara. I have some torn dirham I keep in it, along with other shamanistic odds and ends.

A little later our young guide, Mohamed, stumbled upon a 'kosher' restaurant where we had a lovely meal; I was glad to see a few Jews still in Morocco. We continued on our way, then suddenly, Mohamed was gone. We started to panic. We looked everywhere, wandering around a section of the souq where butchers displayed their wares: goat's heads, entrails, sides of meat undefined and buzzing with flies. Wafts of goat crap mixed with dark dust settling all around – where are you, Mohamed? – and I felt that any minute we might come across a nativity scene, in this strange biblical dream.

Finally, as if we had been hallucinating, our mysterious escort reappeared right next to us, as if he had never left our side. He laughed and winked at Breanne, who proclaimed him 'the man with a paper ass.' He led us to a rug merchant who insisted we sit on low stools and enjoy his hospitality while he had his minions drag stacks of rugs to our feet. We sipped the sweetest of all the mint teas ever served, poured dramatically from a hammered silver pot high above into colorful glasses. He pulled out a lighter and demonstrated the purity of the wool, 'You see it does not burn! This is a very fine rug; you will buy it! We will ship it to you, easy breezy. See how I can wrap it so tightly? Maybe you take two – I make a special price!'

I couldn't resist and took them both. (When I finally removed them from the paper six months later, I could still smell the souq, the goat's red dirt and every foot that had ever stepped upon them ... divine!) Finally Mohamed brought us back to the main path that wound back down to the exit. Exhausted, high, exhilarated, filthy and ecstatic, we stumbled back into the new world as if we had been thrown up by the past into the present. After a shower, a cocktail and a lovely dinner, I somehow longed to go back again.

Off the Beaten Path in Guatemala

BRUCE BERESFORD

Bruce Beresford is a film and opera director. He was nominated for an Academy Award for the script of *Breaker Morant* and direction of *Tender Mercies*. He directed *Driving Miss Daisy*, which won the Academy Award for Best Film in 1989. Other films include *Black Robe*, *Crimes of the Heart*, *Double Jeopardy* and *Mao's Last Dancer*. He recently directed André Previn's opera of *A Streetcar Named Desire* for Opera Australia. In 2011 he is directing Carlisle Floyd's opera of John Steinbeck's *Of Mice and Men*, also for Opera Australia.

Los Angeles, 1982. I was there to direct a film and suddenly found myself, because of a sudden coup in the studio hierarchy, with a spare week. My film was put on hold while the new heads decided (a) whether to proceed with it at all and (b) if the decision was made to proceed, would there be, perhaps, a change of director?

I decided that this was an ideal time to make a visit to Guatemala. I had long wanted to see the Mayan ruins at Tikal. This was before the days when travel bookings were laboriously made on the internet, so I visited my local travel agent and bought three tickets for the following day – for myself, my son (age thirteen) and my daughter (age fifteen).

We turned up in plenty of time in an obscure section of Los Angeles airport. All went smoothly until I was asked for our visas. I had been told, I explained, that visas weren't necessary for Guatemala. Quite wrong. Could I get the visas here at the airport? Impossible. They could only be obtained from the Guatemalan embassy in downtown Los Angeles.

Back to our house in Los Feliz. The next morning I was given the address of the embassy and drove downtown early so that I could be there when it opened at, I assumed, nine o'clock.

The address turned out to be in a particularly run-down part of the city. Every second store sold liquor, the streets were strewn with rubbish and the passersby were sadly down-at-heel. It took me some time to locate the correct number of the embassy building and, when I did, it proved to be a huge hole in the ground. I stared at it for some time in an understandable state of bewilderment as this was unquestionably the address given to me by someone on the embassy staff.

After a few minutes a Latino man passing by asked if I wanted the Guatemalan embassy. Many people, he said, came to the address of this huge hole. He couldn't understand why this was when the embassy had moved two years previously. Luckily, he knew the new address and wrote it down for me.

The new 'embassy' was a few streets away. It was just one room in a broken-down office building. Although the room was full of what looked like very disgruntled Guatemalans, slouching in uncomfortable chairs, the visas were stamped into the three passports within a few minutes.

The next day we flew to Guatemala City, rented a car and drove to the old capital of Antigua, which proved to be one of the world's most beautiful cities, having the stunning architecture, gardens, churches, houses and squares characteristic of so many Spanish colonial towns.

I kept hidden from my son and daughter a printed warning I had picked up from the Australian consulate in Los Angeles, urging me to 'exercise a high degree of caution. Guatemala has a high crime rate. Criminals have targeted tourists arriving at the international airport and traveling to hotels in Antigua.'

After a couple of glorious days of sightseeing and meetings with nothing-but friendly locals, we drove back to Guatemala City and caught a small plane to an airport near Tikal. Both the plane and airport reminded me of Howard Hawks' 1939 masterpiece *Only Angels Have Wings,* with its unflattering but vivid recreation of a banana republic. I realized that the Hollywood version of Central America wasn't too wide of the mark.

The one-room arrival lounge quickly emptied of the few passengers, leaving us in the company of a louche black girl. Intending to phone to check on our hire car, I asked, 'Do you have a phone?' (This was the pre-cell-phone era, of course.) Lazily, she reached under the bench she was slumped across and produced a vintage black telephone, covered in dust. There was no dial tone. 'This phone doesn't seem to work,' I said.

'No,' she replied, 'but you said, "Do you have a phone?"'

The hire car arrived a few minutes later. With my son navigating, we headed down an appropriately potholed road towards Tikal. My daughter read from the guidebook a section which strongly advised against staying in the huts at the historic site itself as they weren't clean, the food was terrible, the organisation a shambles etc. I'd decided to risk it regardless as the nearest hotel was so distant.

As is so often the case, the guidebook was in error. The accommodation, though not luxurious, was clean and comfortable, the food plain but tasty and the English-speaking lady who seemed to be in charge of everything associated with Tikal was delighted to have three such enthusiastic guests.

After a few days clambering over the ruins – pretending to my children that I was not terrified to follow them up steep narrow staircases and then to walk along narrow crumbling brickwork with a sheer drop on both sides – the lady in charge of everything asked if we'd like to visit another Mayan city a few miles away. There is no other Mayan city nearby, I smugly assured her, having read all the material on the Maya I could find. I backed this up by producing a local map, which showed no other Mayan city.

She put the three of us in her Land Rover and headed off along a jungle track. An hour or so later we emerged into a large clearing with huge and totally unrestored ruins. A number of men were idly sitting around on the remnants of temples. 'What do they do for a living?' I asked. There were no towns around and no farms. 'They rob tombs,' was the answer.

Friends greeted us back in Los Angeles a few days later with screams of relief. 'We're so glad you're safe,' we were told. 'The coup in Guatemala has been all over the papers and TV. The country is in uproar. Thousands dead.'

Evidently someone with the suitably sinister name of General Efrain Rios Montt had taken over the country, an event that managed to bypass me. We saw nothing.

I seem to be able to march obliviously through turmoil. I was on holiday in Paris during the 1968 riots and was unaware of anything amiss. I was in Enugu, Nigeria, during a military coup in 1966 and noticed nothing out of the ordinary.

Perhaps I have a strange gene from my father, Leslie Beresford. I was told that when he was called up for military service at the outbreak of World War II in 1939 he was stunned that a conflict was imminent. His interests were almost solely Australian Rules Football and cricket. He read only the sporting pages of the newspapers.

Whatever the reason, our introduction to Guatemala was blissfully benevolent and peaceful. Everyone we met had been friendly – except the lady with the phone.

Kala

JIM SHARMAN

Jim Sharman is a stage and screen director of over eighty stage productions, most recently *Così fan tutte* (Opera Australia 2009 and 2012) and films, including the cult classic *The Rocky Horror Picture Show*, and currently *Andy X: An Online Musical*. He is the author of *Blood & Tinsel* (Melbourne University Publishing, 2009).

Sydney 2011. Eli and I sit quietly on a garden step in silent conversation. We often do this. I'm sixty-six and he's six. I'm looking for a point of contact in faraway eyes. I enquire of my godson what he remembers of our shared holiday in Galle Fort on the southern tip of a teardrop in the Indian Ocean known as Sri Lanka.

'The sea turtles ...' Eli recalls, shyly. 'And ...' with a roar '... Kar – luuu!'

>>>>>>>>>>>>>>>

Sydney 2010. My own recollections of this trip began with the news that greeted me on arrival at Sydney airport on June 24, a day of political drama. After an overnight coup, Julia Gillard had replaced Kevin Rudd as the prime minister of Australia. Fellow travelers greeted this turnaround with uneasy silence. As opinion pixelated across plasma screens, one commentator slipped in a sly aside: '... they've thrown another leader on the barbie.'

I'd scheduled a Bangkok stopover before meeting up with Eli and his mother, Aline, at the Galle Fort Hotel. The trip was intended as a triple-treat: it offered respite to Aline, my neighbor and film-producer friend, and renewal for me; for young Eli, it was a free pass into a world beyond his own backyard.

>>>>>>>>>>>>>>>

Bangkok. The view from my hotel room in the newly minted Le Meridien on Surawong Rd was contradictory: ochre-tiled pagoda temples on one side and the eerily deserted twilight zone of neon nightlife on the other. Spirit and flesh were Bangkok magnets, but the city was recovering from riots by red shirt supporters of exiled prime minister Thaksin Shinawatra and even sex tourists were in short supply. I'd flown from an overnight Aussie political coup into the aftermath of a military coup-d'état.

Tom Vitayakul, a friend, an art-lover and a restaurateur, revealed another Bangkok. He guided me through the vertical labyrinth of the Bangkok Art & Culture Centre gallery, a soaring atrium that housed beautifully curated modern art. And we ate. A traditional Thai meal at Tom's Ruen Urai restaurant and, after a market quest seeking hand-sculpted toy animals for Eli, he introduced me to the delights of thousand-year-old Chinese duck eggs. A wave from Tom: 'There you go!' His farewell take on the Thai Buddhist adage, *mai pen rai* – it's nothing.

>>>>>>>>>>>>>>>

Galle. As my flight disembarked at Colombo's Bandaranaike Airport, I was reminded of tropical North Queensland. At 1am the airport seemed provincial, dowdy and slow. I met with Amahl, the perky hotel driver, and we embarked on the three-hour drive that would deliver us to Galle Fort Hotel at 4:30am.

Amahl steered his four-wheel-drive along dimly lit and often potholed roads. Sri Lanka was devastated by a tsunami in 2004 and by a thirty-year war with Tamil separatists that had only recently ended. It was a post-tsunami, postwar reconstruction zone and soldiers had been redeployed into a nocturnal army of road workers. There was a shantytown feel to the place, enlivened by bursts of light from luxuriant temples. Amahl explained that they'd just celebrated the *poya* (full moon) festival. Illuminated temples and the murmur of revelers returning to their villages punctuated our journey.

The shanties soon gave way to the ghostly ocean and the realisation of being on an island under the dominance of the sea. It was easy to imagine ancient deities rising out of these tempestuous tides and demanding worship or sacrifice. We passed Sinhalese revelers partying on a black rock, their flesh silhouetted by glinting moonlight as they swayed and weaved around waves dancing at their feet. I was reminded that islanders know all about the sea – its beauty, bounty and random fury, while tourists simply enjoy the view.

The Galle Forte Hotel is used to nocturnal arrivals and the friendly manager ushered me into a spacious apartment. I unpacked and slid under mosquito netting into the comfort of a four-poster bed. Morning revealed a beautiful sunlit room with a high ceiling; it's fashionably sparse, elegant and meditative. There was a walk-in shower, a desk, discreet wi-fi but no distracting television. It seemed the perfect place to turn thoughts into ideas, and so it proved to be.

Daylight encouraged a post-breakfast stroll to explore Galle Fort, with its trading history stretching back to the Greeks and Arabs and encompassing a succession of Portuguese, Dutch and British colonial eras. They'd all left their mark in blood, stone, culture and architecture along the walled ramparts, narrow mediaeval streets, and terraced cottages housing today's religiously diverse Sinhalese.

The afternoon heralded the arrival of Aline and Eli. The handcrafted wooden giraffe and silk elephant from a Thai market excursion worked their spell. Eli was up and away, brandishing his complimentary ice cream. A relieved Aline relaxed by the pool, reclaiming some of the sensuality that she'd sacrificed to work and child care. Eli, meanwhile, established diplomatic ties with the youngest of the hotel staff,

Kala

the two As: Arjuna (whose name means 'dawn') and Ahmeel ('invaluable').

At dusk, Eli murmured a reluctant bye-bye to the As and accompanied Aline and me on a hike around fortress ramparts at the magic hour, that ultramarine moment before night's curtain envelops black rock promontories and the velvet sea. Scanning this southern ocean, I was reminded of a song: 'Antarctica starts here.'

In the respite days ahead, Aline read, relaxed, swam in the hotel pool. I paced and ruminated in my sun-filled room. Eli treated the Galle Fort Hotel like an adventure playground and, with balloons supplied by the playful As, he was chased, captured and cosseted. There were day excursions where hillside meals alternated with Eli stick-fishing, suspended on wave-defying stilts. Eli was at his happiest releasing baby turtles back into the sea and on twilight rampart strolls, where his tiny footprints landed lightly on ancient battlegrounds. There were wide-eyed stares at death-defying cliff dives by athletic locals and we were joined in nightly meals on fan-cooled verandas by Eli's new best friend, Kala, the hotel dog – lazy, but loved.

Kala, pronounced kar-lu, means 'black'; it's the old Arab word for Galle, named after the harbor's black rocks. Kar – luuu! It's a primal yodel, and the word throbs in your throat. It became Eli's banshee cry as he clambered over ramparts and chased balloons around the hotel before being corralled by Arjuna or Ahmeel and settling into angelic sleep on a foyer sofa.

Eli had two default states. One was as sweet and engaging as the hotcake butter from a Galle Fort breakfast, while the other was full warrior mode: loud, attention-seeking, destructive. His child's world was a silhouette in black and white; more subtle colors would wait in the shadows to be etched in by time.

Kala

The sunlit room, the fort, the island: they ruffled my imagination. It's twenty years on. Eli is twenty-five. Aline is my age. I'm gone. Eli returns to Galle Fort Hotel to relive the sensation of his first encounter with the wider world. Arunja and Ahmeel now run the modernized hotel. They're middle-aged. The two As try to recall a rambunctious kid they once chased with balloons. They can't. Galle is now a busy town and the once shanty-strewn road from Colombo is a neon-lit, apartment-flanked highway. Galle Fort is an international tourist mecca.

>>>>>>>>>>>>>>>>>

Sydney 2011. We sit on a step in a Sydney garden and Eli's cry jolts us back to teardrops past. Adventurers return with treasure from their travels and Eli's bounty is a single word – Kala. It conjures distant forts, enchanting hotels, animals, rocks and sea; its sound throbs and pulses across time ...
'Kar – luuu!'

Goods and Chattels

JOHN SEALE

John Seale, AM, ACS, ASC, was born in 1942 in Warwick, Queensland, and now lives in Sydney, Australia. He has worked internationally as a cinematographer for over thirty years. Three of his films, *Witness*, *Rain Man* and *Cold Mountain*, were nominated for an Academy Award, and a fourth, *The English Patient*, won an Academy Award, a Bafta Award and a European Film Award. His other films include *Gorillas in the Mist*, *The Talented Mr Ripley*, *The Perfect Storm* and *Prince of Persia*. He has been awarded an honorary master of arts from the Australian Film Television and Radio School, and an honorary doctorate from Griffith University, Queensland, and in 2002 he was appointed Member of the Order of Australia (General Division).

John Seale

For over thirty years I have traversed the world – visiting all its continents and crossing all its oceans, making camp in remote corners and drowning in the excesses of its biggest cities.

Seldom have I had any destination choice. As an Australian freelance cinematographer working mainly on international feature films and with the insecurities of continuity of work, I felt compelled, every time the phone rang, to say 'Yes' to any job offers. Locations for filming are usually selected by the director and/or the producers and their choice is quite often determined by costs and production budget.

My wardrobe was always on standby to 'snatch-and-go' – from arctic subzeros to searing desert highs, from muddy campsites to five-star resorts. I learnt early to minimize my pack of clothes and possessions – difficult when sometimes the film schedules could extend for six months or longer. And particularly difficult when you decide to pack up and take your wife and children too!

In the early '80s I was working on a film that was being shot around Saint John, New Brunswick, in northeastern Canada. The location was selected for its superb fall colors and we rented a log cabin there on the Kingston Peninsula. As the weather cooled down and the trout lakes froze over, our 'Australian' wardrobe was subsidized with layers of Canadian warmth. The children were attending the local elementary school and, as it was hunting season, they had to wear bright orange Day-Glo vests to walk through the woods to their school bus. During our months there they found many treasures they loved and just had to keep.

We left Saint John in a severe November snowstorm and flew directly to New York.

New York was having an unseasonal heatwave. We had to attend a black-tie function and the airlines had lost one of our bags. Of course it was my wife's, and the children were complaining loudly about the New York heat. Then it was on to Miami for gear checks for the next movie, which was being shot in Central America. With no time or funds to return to Australia for a repack, we 'filled in' ten days on a rental yacht out of Hopetown in the Bahamas and then flew on to Belize for the next five months.

By now we had accumulated many bags with schoolbooks, souvenirs and treasures, snow gear and hunting vests, black tie and glam gowns, Christmas presents and snorkels and flippers, violins and light meters, jungle boots and sandals, fishing lines and maps and malaria tablets, lots of suitcases and lots and lots of dirty washing. A mountain of possessions – a nightmare!

That was when we brought in the family 'you can take whatever you want – but you have to carry it' rule.

Our children are now adults and flexible and confident travelers of this earth. Their years of struggling with gear and complaining about the weather and wanting to be at home for a friend's birthday party are over. They know how to pack in a hurry, to minimize and to anticipate what gear will be required. They have tasted and enjoyed foods from many cultures and have the extraordinary ability not to get lost in a strange city. I guess these are lessons that can't be learnt in a classroom.

Meanwhile I still drag home too-full suitcases from around the globe. Another coat when I am cold, a bundle of scripts to read, my treasured yachting magazines and, of course, the odd piece of boat hardware – a bargain found in some dusty corner of the world. I have been known to leave out a bag of dirty laundry to make room for these treasures ...

I tell everyone else who is packing up to travel somewhere – 'less is best.'

But sometimes even I forget.

Glides Like a Piano

ANTHONY EDWARDS

Anthony Edwards has been a professional pretender for the last thirty-three years. Most people remember him as Goose in *Top Gun*, Gilbert in *Revenge of the Nerds* and Dr Green in *ER*. He's the father of four kids and husband to one wife. Born in Santa Barbara, he was the youngest of five children. His parents instilled a need for travel at a very early age. Anthony dedicates free time to www.shoe4africa.org, an organization that uses sport as a way to bring about health and educational change in Africa.

What would happen if both engines quit?
'Don't worry, it glides like a piano.'

That is not really what you want to hear about a plane that is going to take you and your family around the world for a year. But Len Riley, our pilot, also communicated without words, by way of a grin and a knowing look of assurance, that it was his job to never let us be in a situation in which gliding like a piano was an option. He and his copilot, Orlando Moreno, would take care of the flying. I could look at this trip with fear, dwell on the worst case scenario and become paralyzed with inaction – or I could trust, look at the big picture and focus on the fact that this was going to be the adventure of a lifetime.

We are a family with four children. In the fall of 2006, our youngest, Poppy, was four, Wallis, five, Esme, nine, and our oldest, Bailey, was twelve. My wife, Jeanine, had created, built and sold a very successful makeup company. I had spent eight years being the well-intentioned, bad-luck Dr Green on *ER* and we now lived in New York. With our oldest going to high school pretty soon, this was the moment that we as a family could take a year off to go around the world. Six in our family and two teachers made a party of eight that needed to travel to thirty countries in 310 days.

Len Riley was the possessor of the grin and knowing look of assurance that made him the quiet foundation of this trip. He was a pilot who grew up in Alaska and would 'borrow' planes as an underage teenager, like a 14-year-old in the lower forty-eight would sneak out in his dad's car. He was born to fly. Being around someone who is doing what they truly love is inspiring. And that is why when we asked Len if he would be interested in this adventure, there was no surprise when he lit up and said, 'Yeah, I think I can do that.'

We left New York's Westchester Airport in a twelve-seat Challenger 601 packed to the gills with suitcases, books, crafting materials, instruments, even an 88-key keyboard (which was given away pretty early in the trip as we realized that piano lessons were going to have to be put on hold). We did look a bit like the Clampetts heading out to Beverly Hills – actually more like the Clampetts after they had been in Beverly Hills, bought a plane and thought they would take their life on the road for a spell.

Our kids were all in a Waldorf school, which has a curriculum that is based around the idea that in educating a child, reading, writing, math and the sciences are to be explored using the mind, the heart and the hands. With the help of two great teachers, we were able to integrate that idea into the itinerary of our trip. The seventh-grade curriculum uses the Renaissance as its foundation and so after a dramatic and spiritual visit to one of the wonders of the world, Machu Picchu, we zipped over to Florence to start our school year in the heart of the Renaissance. Wallis turned six in Italy and I think she thought that this trip was going to be just fine because all the ice cream around the world was going to be that good. This was going to be a great year. We had a lot of birthdays ahead of us.

Our plan of what to see came from a few sources. We discovered that the 'Seven Wonders of the World' are very open to interpretation. There are the natural wonders and the man-made wonders. We combined them and ended up with Machu Picchu, the Coliseum, the Acropolis, the Pyramids, the Serengeti, the Taj Mahal, the Ganges, Angkor Wat, Uluru (Ayers Rock), Kyoto, the Great Wall of China, Lhasa and Petra, among the most famous. We also used the '1000 things to see before you die' theme, which got us thinking about festivals and certain-times-of-the-year events such as Tet in Vietnam, the migration in Africa, the Ice Hotel in the Arctic Circle, the religious rituals of the monks of Luang Prabang, Hindu festivals in India, the Buddhists of the Himalayas, Balinese temples and Ramadan in Cairo. This year was about going far away. We were very lucky to have time and this plane that we could use like a Winnebago. We never had to worry about connecting flights, luggage limits and lost bags, and we could stay as remote as possible.

As a father, you always want your family to be safe. Learning and growth that can come from traveling require some venturing into the unknown. Spontaneity and surprises stimulate and challenge expectations, which leads to new perspectives. This adventure was going to take us to pretty remote parts of the world. An international health doctor can fill you with all kinds of fear in relation to infectious diseases, vaccinations and lack of access to care. It was always reassuring to know that Len, Orlando and the plane could get us on our way to a medical center as soon as we could meet at the airport.

Be prepared for the worst but enjoy the best: that is what I respect most about good pilots. They have a great deal of respect for the power of weather. They understand the limits of the machines that they fly. Big mistakes are usually a result of lots of smaller mistakes adding up to failure. The details are never overlooked. When they are doing their job right, it seems effortless and smooth. They give themselves every opportunity for success.

One of our destinations was the small Himalayan country of Bhutan. Its remote, high-altitude airport has only one approach to land and it is not in a straight line. As we descended between the snow-covered peaks into a series of turns in which the highest mountain range on earth seemed to be in spitting distance outside our windows, I looked up to the cockpit where

Len and Orlando appeared relaxed and focused. Now I understood why three weeks earlier Len and Orlando had been in a flight simulator flying this approach over and over again to get the certification to land in Bhutan. No surprises when you only have one first time. Always be prepared. Good pilots don't experiment and explore with a family in the back.

Another challenging aspect of getting ten people around the world is the logistics of international travel. Customs, refueling and airport red-tape are a few of the hurdles. It wasn't that we planned on having to pay off people, but Len was smart enough to know that to have some cash stowed away for an emergency was a good idea. The day we arrived in Ghana, the machine that printed out our visas had a 'mysterious' malfunction after six of the visas were complete. Our choice was to wait until the next day or take the six visas and 'leave the money' for the other four. Two months later, very late at night, we had a scheduled stop to refuel in Myanmar. After a long discussion, Len came back on the plane and made his way to the cash box. Knowing that the country at the time was very unstable, it appeared to be a better idea to not argue the details, give them cash for the gas and get back up in the air as soon as possible. They say that the English brought bureaucracy to India and the Indians perfected it. When we were in India, excessive paperwork – the result of India having so many different air-control jurisdictions and a rapidly expanding airline industry – made what little hair Len had go gray. I never saw him so relieved as when, after a month, we finally left Indian airspace.

Len's voice over the PA system sounded very legitimate, like a commercial airline captain's. During the trip we crossed the equator six times. Every time he would say, 'Ladies and gentlemen, please sit down as we are approaching the equator. We must be prepared for the bump.' The kids' eyes would get a little wider and sure enough the plane would bounce up and down (lightly). There would be a little cheer and then he would look back at us with a big grin and comment on the mysteries of nature.

The only bad flight we had on the trip was when Len was not flying and we had to take a small twin-engine plane back to Johannesburg from a game lodge. As we flew into a big storm cloud and the turbulence literally made bags hit the ceiling, I was thinking Len would never follow a route like that into a storm. The icing on the cake of that horrible flight was that on our descent into Johannesburg, a hawk bounced off our windshield with a thud.

When we left New York in September, we basically knew where we were sleeping through December. So during the first few months while the kids were having school in the morning, Jeanine, the master of the internet, and I would work on the rest of the year's plan. We would first check with Len to see if it was possible to get there, which ninety-nine percent of the time he could make happen, and then continue to fill out the calendar. We also had a fantastic travel agent, Michele Cook, who would always come through when the hotel and house rental logistics got crazy. It was a high-functioning team working out the details and without an internet connection, it would have been virtually impossible.

To find the rhythm of how to live while on a 310-day trip was something we discovered through being a family. Kids are a great barometer as to whether you are doing too much or pushing too hard. The mood swings of exhausted kids in a confined space will quickly make you adjust your expectations. We very soon got into the plan of 'one thing a day.' School in the morning and an adventure in the afternoon worked for us. Your senses and awareness are on a heightened level. The ease and comfort of a typical day at home is not going to happen. I am sure that people get sick when they travel because they just wear out, trying to pack it all in. In the constantly changing environment, we found the effort of slowing down brought more energy to our overall enjoyment of a day.

There was an afternoon when we were in the wilds of the Masai Mara National Reserve surrounded by a large herd of elephants, mothers and babies, taking care of each other and going about their routine, that I saw all of our kids engaged and enraptured, sitting in our open vehicle, not able to speak. The energy was vibrant and the feeling of connection to the magic of the earth tangible. That is why we did this, so we could be consumed by moments where there is absolutely nowhere else in the world where you would want to be.

We wanted to see the world. We wanted our children to experience other cultures from their own perspective. We wanted to make deposits into their memory banks of senses that they could draw from in their future wherever and whenever they needed. Traveling sets the foundation for how to live a life. You must be open and not afraid. Be prepared and smart by thinking ahead. But mostly know that you cannot control everything because the most unexpected thing will happen and you will have to move through the event to find your path again.

On the morning of May 10 in Beijing, China, while the kids were having school, Jeanine got a call from a stranger on Orlando's cell phone that Len had suffered a massive heart attack, Orlando was giving CPR and they were on the Great Wall waiting for an ambulance. We rushed to meet them at the hospital. There was nothing anyone could have done. That was Len's last morning.

The shock, and feeling as if the carpet had been pulled out from under us, was immediate. Our grief was huge and needed to be put to the side for a while, as what was most important was to deal with the logistics of getting Len's remains back to his family. All was accomplished. The embassy was very helpful. Orlando's care as a copilot and friend to Len was deeply compassionate and I witnessed what was truly good in human nature.

Our first impulse was to stop the trip and go home. How could we continue on this adventure without one of our leaders, who had become part of our family? Very quickly we realized that no-one would be more upset about us stopping because of losing Len than Len. He had dedicated so much time and energy to getting us around the world. He had left his life back home to get this done.

We finished the last two months of the trip. Incredible adventures were waiting for us, more sights, discoveries and people who stirred our thoughts and confirmed what an amazingly diverse planet this is that we live on.

I am so thankful that Len's daughter was with him while we were in New Zealand, Australia and Bali. He was so proud of her. I have great pictures of Fran, whom Len was going to marry in June in Greece, riding on a motorcycle with Len in Vietnam with the biggest smile.

The journey of a lifetime was just that, an event that holds in it a lifetime full of observations and experiences. But of course what really stays with you are the shared moments you had with the people you were with. I often think about what brave adventurers my kids were. How lucky I am to have such a smart and loving wife who is my partner in life and cares so much for others' well-being. Two teachers, Molly and Charlene, taught and cared for the kids through the most varied classrooms imaginable. Len and Orlando kept us all safe in the sky and were such honorable men on the ground.

I will never stop wanting my family to be safe while they explore life and push their limits. I often try to imagine how

Len would have done something to make sure that the possibility of success can be maximized.

When we bought the plane before the trip, I remember Len talking about a piece of equipment that it didn't have that he felt was important. It was called a traffic collision avoidance system (TCAS). It was not cheap but Len said that in the very remote chance that we would ever need it, we should have it.

On our final approach, on our last landing coming into Oxford, Connecticut, after 310 days of travel, the TCAS alarm sounded because a small plane was doing acrobatics in our path. The pilots powered on and pulled up. A collision was avoided. All was fine. Len did everything he had promised us. He kept us safe to the end of the trip.

Islands in the Storm

DAN BUCATINSKY

Dan Bucatinsky was the writer and star of the indie romantic 2001 hit comedy *All Over the Guy*, co-starring Adam Goldberg, Christina Ricci and Lisa Kudrow. In 2003, Dan partnered with Kudrow to start Is or Isn't Entertainment, a company best known for its Emmy Award–nominated, HBO series *The Comeback* and its hit NBC docuseries, *Who Do You Think You Are?* now in its third season. In addition to roles on his own shows, Bucatinsky has worked as an actor in dozens of films and television shows, including *In Plain Sight*, *Grey's Anatomy*, *Curb Your Enthusiasm*, *Under The Tuscan Sun* and *The Opposite of Sex*. As a result of his regular performances in *Afterbirth: Stories You Won't Read in a Parenting Magazine*, Bucatinsky signed a book deal with Simon & Schuster to bring his autobiographical tales of parenthood to bookstores by Father's Day, 2012. He lives in Los Angeles with his partner of seventeen years, filmmaker Don Roos, and their two children, Eliza and Jonah.

Having grown up in a city, I've always felt most at home in one. I could say it's because of my sophisticated appreciation for culture – and my need to be near museums and theaters. But I'd be full of it. Truthfully? I've always had a touch of attention deficit disorder and the thought of traveling to a place with large, open, rural farmlands has always made me feel bored and panicky at the same time. I love being a tourist but hate being treated like one. I like walking for hours beyond the grid of a foreign metropolis – losing myself in parts of town where the language and food are strange and delicious and specific only to the locals. But the actual countryside? No thanks. Cities, or towns, or – failing that – small towns. That's my speed.

All that said, when I met my spouse, Don, and he told me he had an old farmhouse an hour north of Dublin, I remember being incredulous: 'Really? How? Or more importantly, why?' After graduating from college, Don had gone to Ireland to fetch and carry (mostly bedpans) for his elderly and soon-to-be-dying great aunt and uncle. They'd lived in a century-old farmhouse in a small parish called Grangebellew. I teased him: 'Why didn't you just get a Eurail pass and a backpack like every other college grad?' But when his relatives finally passed away, Don inherited the house. The joke was on me. Those of us with our backpacks and Eurail passes inherited nothing more than a bad case of crabs from a youth hostel in Avignon.

For some reason, I wasn't eager to visit the house. Having been born of snooty Argentine parents and traveled extensively in South America and Europe, I'd never been attracted to Ireland. It seemed too green and Catholic and – green. But Don had a deep connection with Ireland – the way I had with Buenos Aires – and it was time to see it for myself.

I arrived in Dublin for the first time one early morning in 1995. I looked down from the airplane window as we landed – at an ocean of green farmland that almost instantly filled me with dread and boredom. But then, something happened. After we landed, we drove through the most verdant farmland I'd seen in my life, passing hills littered with sheep and cows and horses. It was so open and virginal. That's right – I said 'virginal.' It was free from high-rises and mini-malls, developments and refineries. And yes, it was green – very, very green. I rolled down the window and drank in the cool, unambiguously clean Irish air. I was in love.

Over the next few years, we traveled to the house in Grangebellew several times. Each time, I would welcome the musty farmhouse smell as opened the front door; the fresh-cut hay, rolled into bales in the back field; the old-fashioned ring of the phone; and even the sad but charming old black-and-white television with only three channels – all of which seemed to be playing *Friends*. We'd sit at the kitchen table enjoying our tea and brown bread, listening to Irish radio. I barely recognized my new self, singing 'Danny Boy' to the cows in the back field, immersed in Irish farm living.

I had such affection for the quaint, yet modest, farmhouse and its rich history as the town's post office for most of the past century. Large stone fireplaces crackled in every room. And there were mysterious stone sheds I'd felt compelled to explore – excavating old wagon wheels, butter churns and milk cans. I'd run upstairs, pull blankets out of the creaky old trunks and smile at the crucifixes that had been hanging on the walls for generations.

One September several years later, we took another trip to Grangebellew and it truly felt like we were coming 'home.' Once we were back in the house, I couldn't stop smiling. Perhaps it was my brain freeing itself from the clutter of life and work and stress, but the air felt cleaner, the sky bluer, the fields greener.

How quickly things can change. The next day, we drove out to Black Rock Beach. The road led right onto the sand. We got out and explored the desolate beach. When we got back into the car, we realized we were stuck. The tires would spin but couldn't move. We were stuck for several hours. I remember feeling like it was the worst possible luck we could ever have. At long last, with the help of a local neighbor, we pushed the car until it finally gained traction again.

The next morning, Don and I decided to take a road trip to Galway. The trip from the east coast to the west would take five or six hours, but we looked forward to driving across the sunny countryside to get there. Around lunchtime, we were passing through the charming township of Cloverhill about six miles from Cavan. Don didn't want to stop. Always the pragmatist about travel, he wanted to eat in the car on the way so we'd make good time to Galway. I'm far more romantic about food abroad: 'I didn't come all this way to eat drive-thru at Burger King!' I scouted the oldest, quaintest looking pub and settled on Olde Post Inn ('They have fig tart!').

We walked along the lunch buffet, piling various kinds of meat, potato and 'veg' on our plates. I glanced up at the television over the bar and noticed a news story about New York City. I looked back down at the peas, carrots and corn in mayonnaise (labeled 'salad') then back up at the television, refocusing my eyes. Unsure of what I had just seen, I pulled Don with me to get a closer look.

'What was that?' he asked. Now everyone in the pub was rushing to look. It was confusing. Had a private plane flown into the World Trade Center towers? At first we thought – as did the newscasters – that it had been some kind of freak accident. Until it happened. Right before our very eyes. We witnessed the second plane fly right into the tower. It was unfathomable. Were we witnessing the beginning of the end of the world? We were on an island so far away – and it was happening across an ocean, on another island, in the city where I was born. I wanted to drop everything and run – the way one does when someone they love is in trouble. Oh how I now wished we'd merely been cursed with the bad luck of pushing our car out of the sand at Black Rock.

Don and I put our plates back down on the table. It was time to go home. But where was home? We raced back to our car, in silence, and drove back to Grangebellew. I tried to call my parents in Brooklyn, but all phone lines to the US were busy. All flights to the US were cancelled. There was no going home.

It was painful to be so far away at a time when our nation was so, well, sick.

I'd always believed the old expression 'Home is where the heart is.' But our hearts were definitely back in the United States, where our families, our friends, our colleagues and our patriotism resided. We were shocked at how the news commentary wasn't as pro-America and pro-Israel as the news to which we'd grown accustomed back at home. It surprised us – and made us even more homesick.

There was a moment of silence planned for the Friday of that week. Everyone pulled off the road. It was touching, but oddly only made me feel more alone. We stopped for lunch in a pub and found ourselves crying at the news reports. A sweet Irish couple came up to us and sympathized 'with our trouble' – the Irish euphemism for a death in the family. Yes. That's exactly what this was. Beyond the literal loss of life, there had been a death – of something far bigger, more profound.

It's ten years later now, and Don and I have two children who have never traveled with us to our house in Ireland. It's time. I guess, whether you're talking about a country or oneself, there's a lot to be said for giving the heart time to heal. Just as the cranes continue to rebuild on Ground Zero, the memory of experiencing that national tragedy from so far away has started to fade. As I plan a trip to Ireland for this coming September – the ten-year anniversary of the 9/11 tragedy – I feel an old, familiar longing for that Irish landscape, the warmth of the people, the smell of our farmhouse. Yes, I feel an almost giddy anticipation about bringing my kids 'home.'

Well, no. Maybe 'home' is not the best way to describe it. I don't think I believe any more that 'home is where the heart is.' I think I've come to feel that home is – just home. And when we travel we are tourists, even to our little farmhouse in Ireland. And that's okay.

Jenifer

JACE ALEXANDER

Jace Alexander is a film, TV and theater director and producer. Among his credits, he directed the pilots for *Burn Notice*, *Royal Pains* and *Warehouse 13*, where he also served as co-executive producer. He has directed several other pilots, and over 100 episodes of primetime TV. Jace is the co-founder of the Naked Angels theater company. He lives in Dobbs Ferry, NY, with his wife, the actress Maddie Corman, and their three children: Isabelle (12), Mac and Finn (both 7).

In the summer of 1992 my best friend Jenifer and I drove across the country, from New York City to Los Angeles. I was heading to film school after an alternate lifetime of being an actor. She was along for the ride, never having seen any other part of the country. On day seven, I accidentally cut off an eighteen-wheeler. When I pulled over to apologize, the trucker, a mullet-haired dictionary definition of a redneck, threatened me with a knife, tried to smash my rapidly closing window, and then chased us, in our boxy Ryder rent-a-truck, for thirty miles across Wyoming.

If Jenifer already felt that anyone from the 'fly over' zone was a potential Jew-hater and killer, well, this cemented that theory. We fought about this all the way to Cody, my eyes pinned, no lights, a dark hundred-mile stretch with a Frogger-like bevy of creatures dashing in front of the speeding yellow truck.

'People and things, just because they're different, aren't all bad!' I screamed, sounding like a Public Service Ad.

'They hate us! I wanna go home!' she shrieked back.

I just couldn't understand that kind of fear. Our entire life was ahead of us, like (pardon the easy metaphor) that long stretch of road. 'We'll be fine,' I told her, but I was really telling myself. Of course, I knew, there was plenty to be scared of. The trick is, keep both hands on the wheel.

In the late winter of 1997, I was a 33-year-old New Yorker whose directing career was just starting to take off. Coming out of the American Film Institute in 1993, I was lucky enough to start directing on *Law & Order*. This led to other TV shows, and by '97 I had steady work in episodic TV. That same year, my aforementioned best friend, Jenifer Estess, was diagnosed with ALS (amyotrophic lateral sclerosis), known more commonly as Lou Gehrig's disease.

Jenifer and I had been close since our freshman year at New York University, but had gotten closer in the nascent years of our theater company, Naked Angels. She was my confidante, my motivator, my right hand. She was my best friend.

I could not, would not accept the prognosis that had been given her: that almost all ALS patients die within five years of diagnosis. I promised her that she'd be different, that together we'd beat it, defy the odds. But over the next two years, she got sicker. The disease started to affect her mobility, and then, her breathing. By late 2000 she was on a full-time ventilator and bedridden. I felt useless and guilty. I was there for her in every way she asked me to be, but I could only watch, helpless, as she began to be attacked from within.

Her sisters Valerie and Meredith, along with her friend and roommate, Julianne, launched an all-out war and formed Project ALS. The organization raised millions and taxed leading scientists to find a cure for the insidious motor neuron disease. At the same time, the Estess sisters decided that a movie should be made that would tell Jenifer's story, and would also help raise awareness about the disease and the work of Project ALS.

Even though by early 2001 I had become a successful TV director, my lack of film credits kept me, initially, from getting the opportunity to direct Jenifer's film. But I fought hard, took meeting after meeting and, with Jenifer's persistent nudging, CBS gave me the job.

Of course, for me, it wasn't a job. It was a mission. I had to give Jenifer, while she was still alive, a film she could be proud of, a film that told her story the way she wanted it to be told.

We went into production in the spring of 2001. Then they dropped the bomb on us: we were shooting in Toronto.

Toronto?! What the fuck?! Jenifer had spent her life in New York City. She was the consummate New Yorker; she couldn't really cook or drive, and anyone who hailed from anywhere outside the Tri-State area was considered 'foreign' and potentially dangerous. And now we had to deal with an entire country of them.

No offense to those nice Canadians, but trolley cars and 'Sorry' every other word and 'oot and aboot' (out and about) just ain't New York City. Of course our prejudices could be assuaged, but this did present some genuine challenges. How could I fake the look of what is arguably the most famous city in the world? How could I get the cast I wanted?

We were told that our cast could contain only five Americans. The Canadian acting union simply never allowed more than that. Ever. But Jenifer wouldn't accept that. There were too many actors that she knew and loved and wanted. So we fought. And we won. By the time we started shooting, we had a cast that included sixteen Americans. No-one has ever done this, before or since.

The cast was unparalleled for a television film. It included Laura San Giacomo (brilliant as Jenifer), Annabella Sciorra and Jane Kaczmarek (as Meredith and Valerie Estess), and a star-studded supporting cast: Edie Falco, Marisa Tomei, Julianna Margulies, Rob Morrow, Fisher Stevens, Camryn Manheim, Vincent Spano and Scott Wolf. My wife, Maddie Corman, played Julianne, and my mother, Jane Alexander, played Jenifer's mother.

On my first day, I shot a couple of scenes on Queen Street. It seemed like a good idea, as it had the life and bustling nature of a New York City street. However, I took a lot of flak for featuring the occasional trolley-car cable. These days it's an easy CGI paint-out, but back then it was a bigger deal. The irony of being told my film didn't look 'New York-y' enough by the very execs who had forced me to shoot the project in Canada was ... Well, network executives, I was to learn, are not big on irony.

Generally, there are some incredibly talented crew folk up in Toronto. However, the pool is small and if it's a busy time, it gets even smaller. For my first Toronto shoot (I would later wind up shooting two pilots up there that were both picked up for series), I was handed a mix of the talented and ... the not so much. But for someone used to the pace and hustle of New York crews, I was a bit flummoxed. As Jane Kaczmarek quipped, 'Those Canadians, ya know, they really go for the bronze ...' Of course, she was only kidding. But, if my first assistant director said 'Sorry' one more time, when there was absolutely nothing to be sorry for, I was gonna deck him.

Once I got over the initial anger and bitterness, however, I discovered that Toronto is an amazing town. It's got great restaurants and great museums. It's got a tremendous wealth of locations. It's got Lake Ontario with its many miles, um, kilometers, of shore front. And people really are a lot more polite.

It was a dream job, and I felt like there was no other human besides me who could have directed her story. I put every ounce of my being into making sure that it was everything Jen had hoped for. I've never worked that hard on anything else in my life. It was my gift to her, just as the opportunity to helm it was her gift to me. But the shoot was far from easy. We had very little money or time, and I had constant fights with the studio. I was young, and yes, it was my first film. But I knew exactly what I wanted, and I knew how to get great performances and tell the story Jen wanted to tell.

I just had to get the execs from the studio off my back. One day, after an exec I'll refer to as 'Dragon Lady' insisted that I consult her before checking the gate and moving on in any given shot, I made a calculated move; I brought her into an adjoining room within earshot of the cast and crew and exploded. I raged at Dragon Lady to 'Get the fuck off my back' and let me make my film. I screamed and cursed and threw a chair, making as much of a noisy display as possible. Dragon Lady left me alone after that. Until editing began. But, that's another story.

The end of this one is: Jenifer died two years after the film aired. I couldn't save her. None of us could. But she lives on, in so many ways; Project ALS continues to raise millions, and she is remembered constantly by the many, many people who loved her and her luminous spirit.

And though I choose to remember Jenifer as the young, vibrant force of life who bounded down Upper West Side streets arm in arm with me night after night, there is another lasting image: at the end of the film, which was simply titled *Jenifer,* the camera pans from a television screen that has just played the last scene of the very same film. It continues to pan across the room and settles on Jenifer, flanked by her sisters, watching the final frames of her own life story.

We shot that one in her New York City apartment. The view looked down on Seventh Ave, and St Vincent's Hospital, where, only weeks later, there would be hundreds of signs and memorials posted by the loved ones of those lost on 9/11. But today it was perfect New York, crisp and sunny and hopeful. The camera lingers, just for a moment, on her face. And even through Jenifer's plastic ventilator, you can see her smile.

Life is a River in India

BRETT PAESEL

Brett Paesel is the author of the *Los Angeles Times* bestseller *Mommies Who Drink: Sex, Drugs, and Other Distant Memories of an Ordinary Mom*. She has been published in many national publications, including the *New York Times*, *Los Angeles Times* and Salon.com. She has also developed television shows for HBO, ABC, Fox, Comedy Central, Lifetime Television, WB Television Network and Nick at Nite. Brett blogs weekly at lastofthebohemians.blogspot.com.

I was tired of failing. That's the simple truth and the only reason why I agreed to go river rafting on the Betwa River that afternoon. I'm not physically adventurous by nature. I am physically timid by nature. But I was tired, tired, tired of feeling afraid, anxious and stuck. Which was why my husband, Pat, and I had persisted in taking our two sons to India, on a trip we could no longer afford, in the first place. It helped, of course, that my brother, who was teaching at the American Embassy School in New Delhi, had said that he would pay our expenses once we arrived. A former army ranger, Keir had even offered to take us all on a ten-day backpacking excursion, ending with a stay with an adventure tourism organization known as 'Snow Leopard' on the outskirts of a city named Orchha. I wasn't sure what 'adventure tourism' was when Keir mentioned it in the planning stage of the trip. Now I knew. It meant camping in tents on the edge of an ancient town, bicycling on battered, butt-busting bikes, and river rafting.

I could have passed on river rafting – which was my first response. My body had tensed at the mention of it, visions of jagged rocks and white water churning, tossing our inflated boat in the air while our family of four clung to each other, screaming out to an indifferent God for deliverance. But, I later reasoned, would that really be any worse than our last year in Los Angeles? Pat and I had lost several jobs and declared bankruptcy – all while helplessly clinging to each other in the middle of many sleepless nights as if we were on a life raft, miles from any visible shore.

Another simple truth: the only thing that scared me more than death by drowning was the thought that I would return from my trip to India unchanged, unable to see past what I had previously determined were insurmountable problems. And worse, that having experienced their parents' ineffective response to adversity, our children would grow up feeling defeated before they even walked out the door to face the world on their own.

As we climbed down the worn, pinkish steps of Orchha Palace to the launch site that afternoon, I was determined to model bravery and adventurousness to the children. I promised myself that I would not inspire new fears in my sons by laying bare my own. Our guide, Vinod, and five guides from Snow Leopard readied a large inflatable raft and the accompanying two-man banana boat. The men in the banana boat, called so because it was shaped like a banana, would come to our rescue if needed. Vinod had been our main guide throughout our stay and had a genial air as if everything secretly amused him and he couldn't wait to tell his wife about it later.

When we reached the pile of life jackets on shore, I said confidently, 'Okay, kids, let's strap these babies on.'

'Babies?' asked my seven-year-old, Murphy.

'Life jackets,' I explained. 'We have to wear these babies in case we fall in the water. Which probably won't happen because these men are trained experts. But in the event that one of us falls overboard, we need to fasten these babies tight so that we're nice and safe and don't drown.'

'Overboard?' said Spencer, eyes widening.

'Unlikely,' I said. I turned to Keir. 'Keir, you're a former army ranger, wouldn't you say that falling overboard is extremely unlikely?'

Keir shrugged, 'It's pretty gentle. What would you say, Vinod? Difficulty, one?'

Vinod gave Spencer a relaxed smile, 'Difficulty zero.'

Spencer cocked his head, unconvinced. I could see my precocious ten-year-old assessing the risk-to-safety ratio with the skills he'd just absorbed from his latest math unit.

He was about to ask Vinod another question when I quickly interjected, 'See, kids? Very gentle waters. But just in case, let's make sure our helmets are secure.'

'I've already checked them,' said Pat. 'We're good.'

'Excellent,' I said and turned back to the kids. 'That way, if you fall out and slam against a rock, you won't damage your brain. These guys know what they're doing.'

'Let me adjust your helmet,' Pat said to me. Now that he mentioned it, the helmet did feel like it was resting on the back of my head, leaving my frontal lobes vulnerable. As Pat fiddled with the straps, he whispered through a fake smile, 'Chill on the bad-stuff-that-can-happen-to-you talk. You'll scare the kids.'

It was true. I was overdoing it, but I couldn't help myself. I wanted the kids to be safe without betraying my own terror at the same time.

'Right,' I said, locking eyes with Pat but playing to the kids. 'Got it, captain. Easy breezy. We're cool. Too cool for school. Give me some of that back, Jack.'

Vinod stepped into the raft. 'Okay. One at a time.'

'One at a time, kids,' I repeated. 'Otherwise we could tip the whole thing over.'

I stepped into the boat, 'Whoa, careful, kids. A bit wobbly at first. And, Vinod? This fabric that is the bottom of the boat must be durable, yes?'

'It's very safe,' he smiled.

'See kids. Super safe. So don't worry about a razor-sharp rock piercing through it and slicing your foot to the bone.'

Pat grabbed my wrist with intent as he stepped into the boat.

'Right. Right,' I said to him pre-emptively. 'I'm done.'

When we were all aboard, Vinod positioned us on the inflated sides. It took effort to maintain balance and I had to grip the boat with my ass to stay upright as a couple of guides pushed us out onto the water. I glanced at Spencer behind me. His gaze was focused but the muscles in his face were relaxed. Vinod's confidence had obviously assuaged his misgivings. Across from me, Murphy's face was open, anticipatory. Good, I thought. They seemed completely unaware of dangers that I knew would present themselves once we encountered white water.

Vinod handed out the oars. 'Be sure to hold onto the handle like so,' he said. 'If you don't, the oar can slip and hit you in the face. We saw a man lose his teeth. The oar slipped loose and smashed them out.'

Jesus Christ, I thought, we haven't even hit the rapids yet and we could lose our teeth? I looked back to see Murphy holding his paddle the wrong way. Keeping my voice even, but firm, I said, 'Did you hear that, Murphy? A man smashed his teeth out. Hold the handle, not the oar part.'

'Like this,' said Spencer with a surprising amount of confidence. Murphy looked at Spencer's hand and adjusted his own. I exhaled.

'Now,' said Vinod, 'when I say 'row,' we row together. When I say 'stop', bring your oars out of the water.'

'Got it, kids?' I shouted over my shoulder. 'Does Vinod need to go over it again?'

'They've got it, Brett,' Pat said. 'It's not that complicated.'

Within seconds, Vinod issued the first command. I concentrated on keeping the same rhythm as Keir ahead of me on my side. Reach out with the oar and pull. Reach out and pull. Out and pull.

'Stop!' ordered Vinod. Keir lifted his oar out of the water. I lifted mine and quickly glanced back. Pat's oar was out. Both boys had followed suit. Jeez. They really had the hang of this and, so far, no-one had lost their teeth. We drifted for a while and my ass muscles relaxed. I looked to shore and saw huge boulders and the shapes of round-topped towers against the bright sky. The water sparkled and lapped easily against the side of the boat. Here we are in India, I thought – adventuring. I bet that anyone seeing us would think we went on adventures like this all the time. We're that relaxed. I looked at Pat, dreamily scanning the shoreline. Could any picture of an adventuring family be more perfect?

Then. The boat began to bobble. In the distance, I heard rushing water. My pulse quickened, my neck stiffened, and I tightened my grip on the oar handles.

'Row,' said, Vinod, with more urgency than he had before.

Keir immediately stuck his oar in the water and started paddling with vigor. In front of me, the others were doing the same. I sliced my oar through the water. Out and pull. Out. Pull. Out. Pull.

Dear God of everything holy and good. Here it was. White water. What the hell was I doing here? I wasn't trained. None of us were, except maybe Keir. If one of us popped out of the boat and smashed our lifeless body against a boulder after being tossed around from jagged rock to jagged rock like a sea lion being flung by orcas before he was devoured, I would never forgive myself. Why hadn't I thought this through? I had been imagining myself as Meryl Streep in that river movie that I never saw because I knew it would scare the shit out of me. But I knew what she'd be like in it anyway, because she's always sensitive and oh-so-strong with flawless skin. I wasn't Meryl Steep, I was a D-list actor – one of the first idiots to be hacked to death in a slasher movie because I'd gone into the basement without thinking anything through! Why hadn't I thought this through? What was I doing in the fucking basement?

From nowhere, the water started to rise and rush ahead, carrying the boat forward. There was no way we could stop now. The roaring river had a momentum that could not be tamed by our flimsy oars. Jagged rocks jutted out of the churning water. Waves slapped against every surface – boat, rock, oar. Water sprayed into our faces. I couldn't see. We crashed up and down. Up and down. Oars struck rocks. How were we hanging on? I didn't know. I couldn't feel my ass. It had been the only point of contact between the boat and me. For all I knew, I was no longer sitting. I wanted desperately to bargain with God, but I couldn't think of words. Up and down. Couldn't form a thought. Up and down. Up and down. Thank you, Jesus – I was still in the boat. The children must be too, unless no-one wanted to scream bad news at me over the pounding current.

And soon. Very soon. Calm.

I held my breath and listened for more rushing water. My skin prickled. I could smell my own fear.

'Stop,' I heard Vinod say. We all lifted our oars out of the water, my pulse still pounding.

'Whoo-hoo!' whooped Spencer behind me. 'That was fun! Let's do some more!'

'Yeah!' shouted Murphy.

What? That was it? How did it get so quiet, so fast? The boat drifted. The two men in the banana boat up ahead smiled back at us. I turned around to see the kids beaming, barely damp from the spray. Pat and Keir smiled like they'd just finished a satisfying meal.

'You see?' said Vinod. 'Difficulty, zero.'

Difficulty zero? What was a 'one,' I thought? Niagara Falls? I looked back at the water we had just navigated. I had to admit that it looked like a very wide babbling brook, a couple of birds perched comfortably on small rocks. How could I have so misjudged the experience? Had my inherent fear about anything more physically challenging than leaning over to pick up a dropped potato chip altered my perception that radically?

'Row,' I heard Vinod say. 'We can stop on shore here.'

Thank God. Land was exactly what I needed. Time to pull myself together before the next rapids. I dipped my oar into the rippling water and reached and pulled with the others. I had known all along that I wasn't the river-rafting type, I told myself. Maybe I should accept my limits rather than push past them. I didn't have to be victimized by my limits like I was in the past. I simply needed to respect them. Make friends with them. After all, my lack of youth, height and glossy hair limited my ability to make a living as a supermodel. Sometimes recognizing your limits was healthy and reasonable.

We pulled the raft ashore and Vinod told us that we would find the ruins of a seventeenth-century hunting lodge at the top of the hill. We followed him up an overgrown path. The ground felt solid beneath my feet. I liked this. I knew this. History. Ruins. Dirt underfoot.

In barely ten minutes, we came upon a couple of turrets flanking a small room. There was a fire pit in front and a shrine to the Hindu god Rama off to one side, newly painted orange. Clearly the lodge was still occasionally used by campers or hunters. The shrine looked so matter of fact and I was impressed, afresh, by what I had noticed earlier in the trip – the Hindu blending of the quotidian with worship.

'Up here!' Vinod called down from what appeared to be a concrete or stone mound about ten-feet high. 'You can see the river.'

Murphy scrambled up to join him. I glanced at Spencer. Ever since he was a toddler, I had anticipated his fear of heights. He had difficulty even climbing a short slide on the playground. Through the years, I had looked at play structures and immediately assessed, 'He's never going to make that.' I had watched him place a foot on the bottom rung, stare up at the monkey bars, and freeze. When we rode escalators, I had to lock eyes with him so that he didn't accidentally look down. Each time, every time, he balked or gave up entirely, his head hung heavy with defeat. At every new challenge, my heart had skipped a protective beat as I struggled with how to soften his disappointment with himself. This is where I found myself. Poised to comfort, I stepped forward.

Spencer stepped onto the rock. I stopped. He timidly reached out one hand to guide himself. I wanted to move further forward, offer him my arm or a boost. But his face had a look of steely determination. He put his other hand down and raised his other foot, placing it next to the other. Now he had both hands and feet on the boulder. Scaling it like a land crab, he started to inch his way up.

'You can totally see the river, Spence,' Murphy crowed from the top, hanging onto Vinod's hand. Spencer lifted his head toward Murphy and smiled, stretching out one hand and then the other, then lifting and placing one foot, then the other. I watched, breathless. Pat appeared beside me.

'He's doing it,' he whispered.

'By himself,' I whispered back. 'Why now? Is he hyped from the rapids?'

'Maybe. I wouldn't exactly call them rapids.'

Spencer reached the midway point, stopped, and looked up again. I started to reach out. This was surely where he'd buckle. Turn back. Look for me. I readied my reassuring smile. But he didn't look back. He inhaled and moved his hand forward again. I dropped my hands. Holy shit. He was going to do it! Maybe he'd finally had enough of being afraid. All eyes were trained on him as he painstakingly inched up the last couple of feet. When he got close to the top, Vinod reached out a hand and pulled him to the summit. Pat, Murphy and I erupted into cheers and applause. Pat hugged me, Murphy pumped the air with his fist, and, teetering, Spencer turned to look down at Pat and me with a goofy grin. If our guides were confused by our familial enthusiasm for such a simple act, they didn't betray it. Perhaps they had children too.

Pat and I scrambled up to meet the boys and Vinod. We gazed over the Betwa River, aglow with triumph. It was a cosmically invisible victory. But the four of us savored it. Spence had climbed a mountain, and in a year when almost everything that could go wrong, had – we had made it to India.

This is where the story should have ended. Neatly. The metaphoric mountain summited. The boy having pushed past his fear and won. The mother having learned that limitations are constructs of our own making and can, therefore, be transcended by the same maker. But had the story ended there, the mother might have thought later that such a triumph was unique to her oldest child. Perhaps it was simply *his* story, she might reason. Perhaps he was simply an extraordinary child.

Our descent was unremarkable and took five seconds. Keir lifted the boys down and they loped ahead, leading the party to the boats. The moment on the rock had been so perfect that I wasn't anticipating angry rapids around the bend. I was, at last, where I should be – on an overgrown path in India, with my family.

Murphy stopped abruptly, turned, and said, 'Dad ...'

His tone was plaintive. I wasn't aware of what was happening but Pat leapt ahead, barking, 'Yank 'em down. Yank the pants down.' He made exaggerated pulling gestures in the air as he hurtled down the hill. For days, Murphy had been suffering the unavoidable intestinal distress that attends almost every foreigner in India.

I sprinted ahead, only to find Murphy staring up at both of us, his legs already wide apart. The look of misery on his face was so complete, so unguarded, it could only be owned by a seven-year-old boy.

He looked up at us, his pants still secure at his waist, and whimpered apologetically, 'I pooed.'

'I know, buddy. I know,' Pat said, leaning down. I stood behind him, seeing Murphy's curly blond hair as Pat eyed him. My body ached with cellular memory, a lifetime of petty humiliations, each one endured, shamefully, not to be spoken of – loose bowels, a period stain, a crush announced to all my friends, a subpar SAT score, a one-night-stand zipping up his fly without a word, a credit card denied by the cashier, a dinner invitation including everyone but not me, bankruptcy. How do we ever move on?

Keir caught up with our Indian guides in tow, the sides of his mouth twitching. He loves a good story about events going horribly wrong, and I could see him already drafting this one. My own mouth hardened protectively. In response, he turned to the men and said, evenly, 'There has been an incident.'

They nodded formally and stepped back a polite couple of paces as if they had just served our meal at a five-star restaurant. I squatted next to Pat, 'Buddy, we've got to take your pants off.'

Murphy squeezed his eyes shut, 'No.'

'Honey, you can't keep them on,' I coaxed.

He stood rigid, like he was growing roots into the soil. As if the very act of staying completely still with his eyes clamped tight would transport him somewhere else. I inferred all of this because I was familiar with the state. I have never been successful at astral projection, but it isn't for lack of trying.

'Honey,' I said, 'you will feel better when we clean you off.'

Without opening his eyes, he whispered, 'I'm so embarrassed.'

'Oh, my love,' I said, 'things like this happen to everyone. Even to grown-ups. No-one thinks anything about it.'

Platitudes, but I didn't know what else to say. Anything further would highlight the fact that there were ten people simply standing around waiting for him to make a move. I breathed in and stared into the distance. Spencer looked away respectfully, sympathy in the curve of his shoulders. I felt stuck. Stuck again. How could I move Murphy from this spot without making him feel worse? I could see Pat sifting through options in his head and I hoped that he had better ones than me. None of us even had a sweater to tie around Murphy's waist.

Murphy's despair made the back of my eyes hurt. He was the littlest. It wasn't fair. He knew it wasn't fair. Spence got to conquer a mountain and Murphy got to shit his pants. Where was the justice in that? There was no story of transformation here – short of his shit turning to gold.

Pat put his hand on Murphy's shoulder. 'We're going to walk down to the river,' he said. 'Then we'll take off your pants and wash them. And we can clean you up too.'

Murphy squeezed his eyes tighter, 'No! I can't move.'

Spencer shifted his weight. My legs were beginning to feel the stress of squatting but I didn't want to move. I thought that standing would indicate impatience. I needed to let him know that we understood how difficult this was. The men behind me waited. We all waited.

'Buddy,' Pat said, softly, 'I'm going to hold your hand and we're going to walk down to the river.' Pat sounded sympathetic but firm. I, myself, had always responded well to this tone. It allowed me to abdicate all decision-making and leave it in the hands of someone who sounded more rational. More capable. The fact that the tone might not match his actual problem-solving capabilities was irrelevant in the moment. Someone had to take charge.

Murphy opened an eye, 'Okay.' He slipped his hand into Pat's. Pat stood up and they started their slow progress toward the river's edge. Either afraid of leaking or simply trying to avoid discomfort, he would not bend his legs or alter his stance. He moved as if he were a human compass, leaning on one leg so he could swing the other stiff leg forward, then repeating the move on the opposite side. The rest of us inched along quietly, not wanting to affect the delicate balance of trust and will that the task demanded.

When we got to the water, I slowly inched down his pants and underwear. Pat and I kept murmuring, 'You're doing great, buddy. You really are.' When we finally wormed his unbending legs out of the soiled clothes, I rinsed the pants in the river while Pat held Murphy's hand and led him into the water, splashing it up to his waist to get him clean. Murphy gritted his teeth, enduring the cold, not looking at any of the bystanders. 'You're doing great, buddy. You really are.'

I wadded up Murphy's wet pants and stuck them in the boat. Murphy, helmet and life jacket still in place, was completely naked from the waist down. Except for his shoes, which Pat slipped onto his feet when he emerged from the river.

'Okay,' said Pat, 'I think we're ready.'

Murphy turned to the assembled poker-faced group and fixed his own face with an expression that looked almost regal – dignified and aloof. As if in response to an unvoiced command from the boy king, everyone jumped into the boat, took their positions, and grabbed an oar. The two guides in the banana boat started rowing ahead of us. Pat led Murphy to the boat and lifted him in. Wordlessly we all adjusted our positions. Murphy picked up an oar and we pushed off.

I heard the water rushing up ahead, but this time I was so focused on Murphy that my body barely tensed. I was empty of any feeling but ache for the boy. Murphy was sitting behind me, bare-assed, and I could feel his humiliation burning through my life jacket. The whole experience had been ruined for him, I was sure. He wouldn't remember the exhilaration of rafting, Spencer's triumph, or standing with his family on a rock in India. He'd only remember that he soiled himself in front of everyone. I was stupid for having agreed to river rafting. If we had been back at the campsite, I could have rushed him to the bathroom or we would have had a clean pair of pants.

The guide in front of me started rowing faster. We kept pace. I didn't look back. We hit the rushing water and used the oars to steer between the rocks. We bobbed and I could hear Spencer whoop. Rowing took all my attention and that was a relief. Muscles moving. Pulling the oar. Pushing away from the rocks.

After a minute or so, there was calm.

'Stop,' said Vinod. Oars out of the water. Keir, Pat and Spencer smiled. I looked back at Murphy, his expression unreadable, his bare legs soaking wet and goose-bumped.

Vinod said, 'Does Spencer want to go into the banana boat?'

I looked at Spencer, reflexively anticipating resistance. 'Sure,' he said, tentatively.

'I want to go,' interjected Murphy. I looked at Pat. Was he going to say it? 'But you have no pants, son.' Had Murphy forgotten already? What was he thinking? I glanced back at my young son. He was smiling, already imagining himself in the banana boat. Had his embarrassment already faded? Or was rowing in the banana boat like his brother simply more important than pantlessness?

'Yes,' Vinod pronounced. 'Spencer, then Murphy.'

The banana boat pulled up beside us and one of the guides stepped onto our boat effortlessly. We bobbled slightly. Instead of feeling anxious, I felt my body give in to the rocking of the boat. Then Spencer stood stiffly. Conducted by two of the men, he made his way haltingly to the front of the raft and was lifted down to the smaller boat.

The many pictures I took of Spencer in the banana boat substantiate my zeal to capture his awkward grace and determination. When it became Murphy's turn, however, I slid the camera into my pocket so he wouldn't be self-conscious as he was lifted up – sunlight bouncing off his bare ass like a beacon to anyone who deems themselves incapable of surmounting obvious obstacles.

Spencer might never be able to articulate why he chose that particular moment in India to climb a boulder. I was even less likely to find out how Murphy decided that missing the adventure would be far worse than his momentary embarrassment. But it reminded me of what I knew already and had forgotten that year: like a river, what propels us forward is far more powerful than what holds us back.

But we must choose it and let go. Every day.